Just the FAQ*s

about the

BIBLE

* Frequently Asked Questions

43

NELSON

FAQ #1

 What Influence Has the Bible Had on Our Society?

 The Bible has played a major role in determining the social values of the Western world.

The Bible has made a monumental impact on our society, and we can be glad it has. During World War II, a South Sea Islander proudly displayed his Bible to an American soldier. "We've outgrown that sort of thing," the soldier said. The islander smiled back and replied, "It is a good thing that we haven't. If it weren't for this book, we would have eaten you by now."

Whether the story is fact or fiction, it expresses a simple truth: If it weren't for the Bible, something, somewhere, may very well have eaten us by now, literally or otherwise. Multiple billions of copies of the Bible have been published to date, and millions more are published every year. While its impact may be diminishing in some circles, it is growing in others, and its historical impact cannot be denied. For example, the United States was founded largely on Judeo-Christian principles drawn from the Bible. When one considers the unprecedented historical impact which this nation has had on the world in the nineteenth and twentieth centuries in promoting peace and political freedom, it is clear that the influence of the Bible extends far beyond the borders of its pages.

The Bible has influenced many societies to adopt important, basic community virtues and to oppose several social vices.

> Give me a Bible and a candle and shut me up in a dungeon and I will tell you what the world is doing.
>
> *Cecil Dichard*

The Family

In some parts of the world, a husband may have more than one wife. She is his property, to treat as he sees fit. In some parts of the world, if a couple produce a daughter when they wanted a son, they simply and literally throw the daughter away. However, American laws governing the family have been forged on quite a different anvil.

The Bible has defined relationships in the family for the last two thousand years. Modern society has largely ignored biblical teachings about the family, and, as a consequence, has seen the family suffer. Yet numerous voices today are calling us back to the ideal, insisting that society flourishes only to the extent that its families flourish.

The Bible's ideal of one man and one woman married for life provides the strongest underpinning for any society.

The Bible's ideal of one man and one woman married to each other for life provides the strongest underpinning for any society. The Bible proclaims the dignity of man, woman, and child. Men and women are equal in the sight of God, and the value of women is upheld in the Christian Bible to a degree higher than that of any other religion's scriptures. The Bible is often misused, and has been falsely accused of demeaning women. Seen clearly, however, nothing could be further from the truth.

Jesus upheld the dignity and equality of women in all His teachings and dealings with women. In Ephesians 5:25, the apostle Paul describes the love that husbands are to give their wives by pointing them to Christ, whose love for the church moved Him to give Himself up for mankind. Total and complete commitment to the wife's welfare is the standard to which the Bible holds all husbands. The apostle Peter writes in 1 Peter 3:7, "Husbands, dwell with [your wives] with understanding, giving honor." Whenever men have exploited women, they have violated the teachings of the Bible.

Jesus held children in the highest esteem. Once, "some children were brought to [Jesus] so that He might lay His hands on them and pray; and the disciples rebuked them. But Jesus said, 'Let the children alone, and do not hinder them from coming to Me; for the kingdom of heaven belongs to such as these'" (Matthew 19:13-14 NASB). The apostle Paul wrote "Fathers, do not provoke your children to wrath, but bring them up in the training and admonition of the Lord" (Ephesians 6:4). Also, in Colossians 3:21 we read, "Fathers, do not provoke your children, lest they become discouraged."

It is true that the Bible has been used to justify the punishment of children with verses such as Proverbs 23:13-14: "Do not withhold correction from a child, / For if you beat him with a rod, he will not die. / You shall beat him with a rod, / And deliver his soul from hell." However, no one can justify the abuse of children on the basis of a Bible quote if he or she knows the whole Bible (not falling prey to the mistake of taking verses like this out of context) and seeks to bring up children in the "nurture and admonition of the LORD." In fact, through the example and teaching of Jesus, children (just as women) are taken more seriously and treated more kindly in the Bible than they are in any other sacred writings. Protection of both the physical and psycho-

Why I Need to Know This

I need to know how important the Bible is...

1. I may dismiss its importance in my life if I underestimate its importance throughout history.

2. I may dismiss the Bible as "just another book" if I don't realize the impact it has had on 2,000 years of civilization. Its extraordinary influence on history requires explanation, and a curious person intent on knowing truth would want to understand it importance.

3. I will miss the opportunity to learn and apply its wisdom in life. We are living in a time when the perceived value of the Bible on society, culture, and individuals is diminishing. I must understand why I should champion the message of the Bible.

logical dimensions of women and children are fundamental responsibilities of all Christian men. That is the origin of laws and customs governing life in America, in spite of all the violations we see.

Labor

Throughout history, the pendulum of conflict has swung between owners and workers, masters and slaves, merchants and buyers, landowners and serfs, or employers and employees. There is a long history of persecution and victimization. The teachings of the Bible, in principle, stop the pendulum swinging. First, it teaches us generally to "do unto others as we would have others do unto us." Second, it teaches us concerning the specific responsibilities of employees and employers:

Slaves, be obedient to those who are your masters according to the flesh, with fear and trembling, in the sincerity of your heart, as to Christ; not by way of eyeservice, as men-pleasers, but as slaves of Christ, doing the will of God from the heart. With good will render service, as to the Lord, and not to men, knowing that whatever good thing each one does, this he will receive back from the Lord, whether slave or free. And, masters, do the same things to them, and give up threatening, knowing that both their Master and yours is in heaven, and there is no partiality with Him (Ephesians 6:5-9 NASB).

Also, in Colossians we read,

Bondservants [applies also to employees] obey in all things your masters according to the flesh, not with eyeservice, as men-pleasers, but in sincerity of heart, fearing God. And whatever

you do, do it heartily, as to the Lord and not to men, knowing that from the Lord you will receive the reward of the inheritance; for you serve the Lord Christ. Masters, give your bondservants what is just and fair, knowing that you also have a Master in heaven (3:22-24, 4:1).

If employees and employers followed these principles, the conflict between labor and management—to see who can take the greatest advantage—would diminish in the workplace.

Race Relations

In some countries, discrimination is accepted and deeply entrenched. Indeed, discrimination among races has been a particularly acute problem in America, although certainly not exclusively. Problems between African-Americans and Caucasians have received the most attention, but conflict among Hispanics, Asians, Europeans, and Eastern Europeans have also been legendary in America. Sadly, it shows signs of worsening in some areas. However, the laws of our country forbid racial discrimination because, as a nation, we believe that all people are created equal in the eyes of God. This value is part of our heritage from the Bible. Scripture lays discrimination to rest. Jesus' teaching of the Golden Rule applies: If we would not like to suffer discrimination, then we should not discriminate. In James 2:8-9, we read, "If [in giving a seat of honor to a rich person] you are fulfilling the royal law, according to the Scripture, 'You shall love your neighbor as yourself,' you are doing well. But if you show partiality, you are committing sin and are convicted by the law as transgressors" (NASB).

These principles were violated in a ghastly display of selective understanding when we tolerated slavery in America. But, terrible as that was, it no longer exists. The breakdown of support for slavery was encouraged, to a great extent, by

The Bible clearly establishes the equality of all people before God.

Christians. Today, no one can claim support from the Bible to discriminate against another person. The Bible clearly establishes the equality of all people before God, and it is a sin to treat anyone otherwise.

Crime

What is lawful and unlawful in America has been influenced significantly by Scripture. Our law says we are not to steal, kill, cheat, or lie. The Ten Commandments also prohibit these acts. According to the Bible, we are not even to covet, hate, or lust! People who aren't well versed in the Bible have stereotypical ideas of what it teaches. It does not teach intolerance, bigotry, and narrow-mindedness. If everyone started following the teachings of the Bible today, most of our major social problems could be well on their way to a solution!

In addition, how we treat criminals is also influenced by the Scripture. Some countries punish thieves by chopping off a hand. Some routinely beat prisoners within an inch of their lives. Some countries exert little to no effort giving a suspect his due process under the law. In America, we attempt to treat everyone as innocent until proven guilty, and then still acknowledge that even convicted criminals have basic rights. These values have grown out of our national acceptance of a biblical worldview.

Humanitarianism

Poverty has always existed and always will. Even Jesus said, "the poor you have with you always" (Matthew 26:11 NASB). Yet the Bible has encouraged our national sense of compassion and directed us to help those in need. Christian organizations have done more for the poor, the needy, and the disadvantaged than any other form of organized help in the world.

The Scriptures, as the marching orders of believers, have advanced humanitarianism more than any other force on earth. From Mother Teresa helping the dying and destitute in the streets of Calcutta, and World Vision feeding thousands in a refugee camp, and the Salvation Army helping the down-and-outers, and the soup kitchens run by a rescue mission, to the church that provides shelter for the homeless, housing for unwed mothers, and financial assistance to those in crisis, Christianity continues to give more to the needy than any other institution or movement in the history of the world. The Bible, both Old and New Testaments, teaches that we should take care of those in our families—the poor, the needy, the hungry—and those who cannot help themselves.

From the earliest days of the church, through the Middle Ages and into the modern age, Christianity has led the world in establishing hospitals, orphanages, and educational institutions. It has led the way in fighting slavery, child labor, and discrimination.

The oldest hospital in existence today is the Hotel Dieu (Hotel of God) in Paris, established by St. Landry around A.D. 600. Christians established the first hospital of the Western world in Rome around A.D. 400. Today, throughout the world, hospitals named St. Joseph, St. Andrew, and St. Anne exist. There are also Baptist, Lutheran, Presbyterian, and Methodist hospitals, testifying to the natural bent of Christian faith toward relieving human suffering and promoting health.

The Bible teaches believers to care for their families, the needy, and those who cannot care for themselves.

Florence Nightingale established the institution of modern nursing out of her Christian compassion. The Red Cross and Young Men's Christian Association (YMCA) were established to extend Christian assistance to the needy. Louis Pasteur, a devoted follower of Christ, advanced medicine into the modern era as an outgrowth of his Christian convictions. Albert Schweitzer, as a result of his desire to serve Christ, helped establish a hospital in a remote part of Africa.

Government

There is no such thing as a "perfect government." But the ideals of government in America, as expressed in our Constitution and Bill of Rights, surpass those of any other government. By contrast, anti-Christian governments, such as the empire of Rome, Mussolini,

Hitler, Stalin, or Mao have been murderous, uncivilized expressions of the darkest corners of evil. The Bible's influence on the establishment of benevolent governments has literally directed international affairs. For example, if the United States had wanted to rule the world, it could have taken control at the close of World War II. After dropping the atomic bombs on Japan, the United States could have said to all other nations, "Unless you want one of these bombs dropped on the doorstep of your capitol, lay down your arms." But it didn't. Instead, it allowed every country its freedom, and even spent billions of dollars helping to rebuild the very nations that waged war against us.

The historic documents of Britain and the United States express biblical principles and spirit.

Christianity has had a profound effect on government in the world, especially in democracies. The dignity of the individual, the establishment of benevolent governments, and the promotion of fair laws are a few of the great legacies from the Bible. It has promoted the humane treatment of criminals and provided a safety net for disadvantaged people. Christianity has had a particularly profound influence on the histories of England and the United States. The major documents—the Magna Charta, the Mayflower Compact, The Declaration of Independence—are filled with biblical principles and spirit. "We hold these truths to be self-evident: That all men are created equal; that they are endowed by their Creator with certain unalienable rights; that among these are life, liberty and the pursuit of happiness." This is perhaps the most lofty ideal in the documentation of all human governments.

Education

Christianity has also been the most powerful force for education in the history of the world. Christianity is a religion of the written word. The Bible is the record of the revelation which God wanted preserved for the good of humanity. Central to the ideal of Christianity is the spreading of education so that people can read and understand the Bible. Many of the languages of the world have been reduced to writing by missionaries so that the Bible could be translated into their language.

Wycliffe Bible Translators, the world's largest Bible translation organization, has translated the Bible for millions of people since its inception. Their goal is to translate the Bible for another three hundred million people who still do not have it in their own language. The primary purpose of this mission is to spread the knowledge of Scripture, but it has the secondary purpose of promoting worldwide literacy.

The first printing press capable of mass production of literature, the Gutenburg Press, was invented to print the Bible, and the Bible was its first publication. It was the passion of the Reformers to put a Bible in the hands of as many people as possible. Many of Europe's finest schools were established to advance Christianity and a knowledge of Scripture.

In the United States nearly every early college was founded for the express purpose of advancing the knowledge of Scripture and salvation. At the entrance to Harvard is a stone on which this inscription is found:

After God had carried us safe to New England, and we had built our houses, provided necessities for our livelihood, reared convenient places for God's worship, and settled the civil government; one of the next things we longed for, and looked after was to advance learning, and perpetuate it to posterity; dreading to leave an illiterate ministry to the churches, when our present ministers shall lie in the dust.

Christianity has been the most powerful force for universal education in history.

Yale and Princeton were founded on the same basic principles. The Reverend John Witherspoon, president of

Princeton, once said, "Cursed be all learning that is contrary to the cross of Christ." Dartmouth was founded to train missionaries to reach the American Indians. The college of William and Mary was established so that "the Christian faith might be propagated." In fact, every college or university in the United States was founded for religious purposes until the University of Pennsylvania was established in 1740.

While colleges and universities have deviated from their original purpose, the Bible continues to play a major role in education in Europe, England, and the United States. In addition, many Third World countries owe their academic heritage to religious education established by missionaries.

If it weren't for the Bible, world literacy would be at a much lower level. Certainly, no other movement in history has exerted such an influence on academia.

In *The Bible and Civilization*, Gabriel Sivan wrote:

More than any other code, past or present, the Bible has urged men and women imbued with a social conscience to tackle the age-old problems of poverty, suffering, and inequality. William Wilberforce fought slavery; Florence Nightingale reformed nursing and Elizabeth Fry prison conditions; Lord Shaftesbury protected the juvenile laborer; Lewis Gompertz pioneered animal welfare; William Booth's Salvation Army redeemed men from the gutter; Jean Henri Dunant made the Red Cross a delivering angel for the victims of war. Millions of underprivileged persons in country after country have been rescued from squalor and misery thanks to the humanitarian instincts and philanthropic work of great idealists [who got their inspiration from the Bible].

FAQ #2

 What Influence Has the Bible Had on Our Culture?

 The Bible has been a dominant influence in the arts of the Western world.

Charles Colson, in his marvelous volume, *Loving God*, told the story of Telemachus, a fourth-century Christian. Telemachus was a peace-loving, beauty-loving man who lived in a remote village, tended his garden and spent most of his time in prayer. One day he thought he heard the voice of God telling him to go to Rome, so he obeyed. Setting out on foot, he arrived in the city weeks later, at the time of a great festival. The little monk followed the crowd down the streets into the Coliseum. He saw the gladiators stand before the emperor and say, "We who are about to die salute you." Then he realized these men were going to fight to the death for the entertainment of the crowd. He cried out, "In the name of Christ, stop!"

As the games began, he pushed his way through the crowd. He climbed over the wall and dropped to the floor of the arena. When the crowd saw this tiny figure rushing to the gladiators and saying "In the name of Christ, stop!" they thought it was part of the show and began laughing.

When they realized it wasn't an act, the laughter turned to anger. As he pleaded with the gladiators to stop, one of them plunged a sword into his body. He fell to the sand. His last words were, "In the name of Christ, stop!"

Then a strange thing happened. The gladiators stood looking at the tiny figure lying there and a hush fell over the Coliseum. In the upper rows, a man stood and

The Christian in tune with Scripture will love the beautiful and hate the morally hideous.

made his way to the exit. Others began to follow. In silence, everyone left the Coliseum.

The year was A.D. 391, and that was the last battle to the death between gladiators in the Roman Coliseum. Never again, in that great stadium, did men kill each other for the entertainment of the crowd.

The Christian in tune with Scripture will love the beautiful and hate the hideous. God is a God of beauty, and hideousness belongs to the devil. Christians ought, then, to be lovers of beauty. Throughout history, Christians have led the world in the creation of beauty through the arts.

Art

The Bible has given art its greatest themes—the creation, fall, and redemption of mankind; the great miracles of the Old Testament; the coming to earth of God as Jesus of Nazareth, born in a manger, heralded by angels, living a life of wisdom, power, compassion, and sacrifice; being killed because of His goodness; His return to earth at some time in the future.

Christian art began to flourish under the protection of Roman Emperor, Constantine, in Byzantium (later called Constantinople and then modern Istanbul) after the first three hundred years following Christ's death. Byzantine art was very flat and representative. During the Renaissance period, the golden age of art was ushered in, and the biblical themes were painted as never before. Michelangelo painted the incomparable Sistine Chapel and carved from stone the *Pieta*, Jesus dead in the arms of his grieving mother, Mary.

Raphael painted hundreds of Christian scenes, including more than three hundred of the Virgin Mary. Leonardo da Vinci gave us the Last Supper, and Rembrandt filled our eyes with the interplay of dark and light, portraying perhaps the most touching scene of Jesus being taken down from the cross after His death.

Books on the history of art prove that Scripture has provided the greatest themes in all of history for art.

In the twentieth century, secularism has caused a profound degeneration in art. Abandoning the images and themes of the Bible, a lot of modern art consciously rejects Christian categories and reflects the debasement of laws, meaning, and morals which typifies our modern society. You can witness the gradual decline of faith just by leafing through a book on the history of art in America. The same holds true for other art forms, as well.

Music

Most great music of the past was distinctly Christian. The haunting Gregorian chant is the focal point of the earliest preserved music. The Reformation brought newly evolving music into the church. Luther's "A Mighty Fortress Is Our God" is the best known example. The Baroque period saw music ascend to heights never before reached. Johann Sebastian Bach (1685-1750) and George Frideric Handel (1685-1759) were devout Christians whose music was composed for the glory of God. Handel's *Messiah* has ministered to millions, and has been performed each Christmas by thousands of orchestras and choirs around the world.

Scripture has inspired the greatest visual art and music of history.

Bach is recognized by many as the greatest composer that ever lived. Much of his music was overtly Christian, with titles such as "St. Matthew's Passion," "St. John's Passion," and "Jesus, Joy of Man's Desiring." Bach often put the initials "S.D.G." on his music manuscripts which represented the Latin phrase *Soli Deo Gloria*, meaning "glory to God alone." Other times he wrote "J.J.", representing *Jesu Juban*, meaning "Help me Jesus." He dedicated some of his works "I.N.J.", meaning *In Nomine Jesu*, or "In Jesus' Name."

Bach's influence was so pervasive that Beethoven, Haydn, Mendelssohn, and Mozart revealed their debt to him in their own musical contributions. It is generally agreed that Bach is to music, what Shakespeare is to literature—each being the highest practitioner of his art form.

Some of the great music masters following Bach were also Christians. But we see, as in art and literature, a steady decline of Christian influence in music from that time to the present. Many music lovers and experts would disagree, but the late Francis Schaeffer, world renowned Christian author and Presbyterian minister, exposed the decline in music, art, and literature as it parallels the decline in overall devotion to God in his book, *"A Christian View of the Bible as Truth."* Bach and others like him, however, laid the foundation for modern Western music. This foundation came from the church and the Scriptures.

Literature

Since the Middle Ages, the Bible's influence on Western world literature is simply immeasurable. Not only has literature drawn upon the Bible as a source for themes and stories, but it has also been heavily influenced by the Bible's images, phrases, and characters. In fact, the Bible's influence on literature is so great that, in the words of the literary scholar, Northrop Frye, "a student of English literature who does not know the Bible does not understand a great deal of what is going on in what he reads." Today, courses in the Bible are offered in many university English departments in order to adequately equip students for their study of literature. Unfortunately many students arrive at college with little knowledge of the Bible.

Read any great work of Western literature from the Middle Ages to the present, and you will invariably discover that the Bible has influenced its subject matter to some degree. Consider a handful of noteworthy examples: Augustine's *Confessions*, the first modern autobiography, tells of the role of the Bible in his own conversion to Christianity. The mystery and morality plays of the medieval church, of which *Everyman* is the outstanding example, enact scenes and themes from the Bible for the edification of worshippers. Both Dante's *The Divine Comedy* and Chaucer's *The Canterbury Tales* exhibit enormous influence from the Bible, as do the works of Shakespeare, John Milton, Edmund Spenser, and many other poets, dramatists, and novelists.

Examples from the last two centuries include the works of Charles Dickens, Nathaniel Hawthorne, James Joyce, Robert Louis Stevenson, Leo Tolstoy, Mark

Twain, Fyodor Dostoevsky, William Faulkner, T. S. Eliot, Thomas Mann, C. S. Lewis, J.R.R. Tolkien, Willa Cather, and Flannery O'Connor. The list could be expanded to include every significant author of Western litera- ture. As scholar Leland Ryken points out, beyond providing major sub- stance to many poems, dramas, or works of prose fiction, the Bible con- tinues to provide titles for works such as *Go Down Moses* (Faulkner), *East of Eden* (John Steinbeck), *The Sun Also Rises* (Ernest Hemingway), and *Go Tell It on the Mountain* (James Baldwin). Many authors draw from the Bible in creating and naming their characters. For example, John Milton transforms the biblical judge in the drama *Samson Agonistes.* Hawthorne derives "Hester" in *The Scarlet Letter* from the biblical "Esther," and the name of her illegitimate child "Pearl" from the "pearl of great price" in Jesus' parable *(The Literary Influence of the Bible,* p. 474). Through such echoes of the Bible, readers are urged to explore both the biblical sources and their relation to the poems, dramas, and stories that use them.

As we have seen in other areas of Western art and culture, the Bible's influence on literature is, in a word, ubiquitous—found every- where at the same time. People who want to understand great works of Western literature must hold in one hand the literature they are reading, but also keep in the other the Bible. Without the Bible, peo- ple not only overlook or misconstrue key elements of literary art, but worse, they are not well-equipped to fully understand themselves or the world around them.

FAQ #3

 What Influence Has the Bible Had on Our Spiritual Life?

 The Bible has been a dominant influence in the spiritual, moral, and ethical formation of the Western world.

The child's game, Pin the Tail on the Donkey, is predicated upon one simple reality. When you can't see, unpredictable things happen.

In a child's game, those unpredictable things are harmless and humorous. In case you are not familiar with the game, there is a picture of a donkey on a bulletin board. This poor donkey, however, is missing its tail. One child is blindfolded, given a tail with a pin sticking through it (I think there are Velcro® versions now), twirled around several times so that he doesn't know which direction he's facing, and told to pin the tail on the donkey. The fun comes when all the children who can see get to watch the misguided attempts of the blindfolded child as he tries to put the tail in the right place. It may end up on the donkey's nose, ear, belly, or even on a sofa, chair back, or between the shoulder blades of an unsuspecting playmate. Much is lost when you can't see.

This game is a metaphor for life. Truth is like light. Ignorance and falsehood are like darkness. With light, living life successfully is difficult. Without light, it is impossible! The fate of civilization hinges on whether or not people will see the light beaming from the Bible and walk in its illuminated path.

Objective Truth

The Bible is important because it gives us objective truth. We are living in a day when some say there is no such truth. In fact, Allan Bloom wrote in his profound book, *The Closing of the American Mind*, that the most common value held by nearly everyone today is that all truth is relative. In fact, if there is one thing that is certain, it is that nothing is certain.

The Bible expresses objective truth.

But do you know what happens if all truth is relative? The blindfold goes on. Suddenly humanity cannot see. It is just as likely to pin the donkey's tail on the sofa as it is on the donkey. It's a dangerous world when you can't see.

The person without truth has no answers for the great questions of life: Who am I? Where did I come from? Why am I here? Where am I going? He has no basis for declaring something right or wrong, good or bad, beautiful or ugly, just or unjust. However, the instant the light is turned on, the danger is over. We see the donkey clearly, and the tail can be put in the right place.

Moral Standards

"Calvin and Hobbes" is a popular newspaper cartoon strip. Calvin is a little boy and Hobbes is his small, stuffed tiger who becomes a large, real tiger when no one besides Calvin is around. One day as they were taking a walk through the woods, Calvin announced to Hobbes that he didn't believe in ethics anymore. As far as he was concerned, the ends justify the means. "Get what you can while the getting's good—that's what I say! Might makes right! The winners write the history books. It's a dog-eat-dog world, so I'll do whatever I have to and let others argue about whether it's 'right' or not."

At that moment, Hobbes pushes Calvin into a deep mud hole. Calvin yells, "Hey! Why'd you do that?"

Hobbes replies innocently, "You were in my way. Now you're not. The ends justify the means."

"I didn't mean for everyone, you dolt! Just me!" screams Calvin as he rises from the wallow, wiping mud from his face.

"Ahh…," replies Hobbes as he strolls thoughtfully away.

Much of Calvin's blood flows through the veins of all of us. We want the freedom to do what we please, but don't want others to have that same freedom if it impacts us negatively. That's why we need the Bible. The Bible gives us moral standards which are necessary if we are to get along with each other. If everyone looks out only for himself, the law of the jungle—the survival of the fittest—becomes the law of the land. Only as people willingly look out for one another can civilization advance. When Jesus said, "Do unto others as you would have others do unto you" (Luke 6:31), He voiced one of the most profound sentences in the history of humanity. With the acceptance of that one principle, many of humanity's greatest problems would lessen.

"If there is no God," wrote Dostoevsky in his great novel, *The Brothers Karamazov*, "then all things are permissible." Evangelical theologian Francis Schaeffer spoke prophetically when he taught that unless you can appeal to God, there is no such thing as right and wrong. You say something is right, I say it is wrong. We cancel each other out. Only if there is a God, and if God has revealed right and wrong to us, can we say something is right or wrong, good or bad, just or unjust.

Hitler killed six million Jews and many Christians who tried to help them. Stalin killed over forty million of his countrymen. Mao was responsible for perhaps as many as seventy million Chinese deaths. All three of these men were committed atheists.

> **"If there is no God, then all things are permissible."**

Without God, the "rights and wrongs" of what we call civilized countries disappear. If there is no God, then there is nothing inconsistent about what these men did. You may not like it. You may prefer that they not have done it, but you cannot call it wrong. But if God calls them wrong, then there is no dispute. They were definitely wrong.

Why do we need the Bible? Because right and wrong, good and bad, just and unjust disappear into a fog of formless gray without the Bible. Unless God has revealed to us a moral code, we have none except that which is imposed upon us by whomever has the most power. Our light becomes darkness.

Life after Death

As we look at the great conveyor belt of life, we see people sitting on it in front of us, and as they get to the end, they drop off. But we don't know where they go. Left to our own knowledge, we have no confidence in knowing what happens when we die.

The Bible speaks convincingly of life after death, and tells us what we must do to prepare ourselves for eternal life. You don't hear much about it these days when tolerance is the number-one virtue, and objective truth is sacrificed on the altar of tolerance, but the Bible teaches that there is a heaven and a hell. Heaven is a place of eternal joy, and hell is a place of torment and eternal destruction.

If the Bible is wrong, then there is no need to worry. But if the Bible is right, there is plenty reason to worry. If you don't like going to the dentist, you will want nothing whatsoever to do with hell.

The Bible teaches that the only thing that separates us from God is sin. All have sinned and come short of the glory of God (Romans 3:23), and the wages sin earns is death, eternal separation from God (Romans 6:23). It teaches that there is forgiveness with God (Psalm 130:4) and that the one who comes to Jesus will not be turned away (John 6:37). The Bible also teaches that those who have Jesus, God's

Son, have eternal life (1 John 5:12). Putting all that together, we conclude that we must come to Jesus, repent of our sins, ask Him to forgive our sins, give us eternal life, and come into our lives and make us the kind of people He wants us to be. That, and that alone, gets us to heaven. How good we are has nothing whatsoever to do with whether or not we get to heaven, because no one can be good enough. We must get there because we turn to Jesus, who will forgive us and give us eternal life if we will give our lives to Him.

Changed Lives

An endless number of people testify to this remarkable fact: Their lives changed when they committed themselves to following the truth of the Bible. Jesus' disciples changed. Many well-known figures throughout history have changed. Millions of people today would say that their lives changed. My own life changed.

My greatest concern about becoming a Christian was that I had turned over new leaves before, but they never stayed "turned over." They always ended up flipping back to their original position. I was afraid of embarrassing myself and of doing God no favors by letting the cat out of the bag and announcing that I was a Christian. Then, losing the momentum of decision, I feared that I would slide back into my old life.

But, when I finally took the plunge to become a Christian, I found a new power, a new presence, a new "something" in my life which the Bible tells me is the Holy Spirit. He would not let me go back to my old life. Sure, I have had relapses, as have nearly all Christians. But something alive within me is always there, pulling me back, convicting me of sin, calling me to righteousness, convincing me of truth, of the validity of righteousness, and the self-destructiveness of sin, making me want to please God and be like Him. My life has been changed by something, and when I read in the Bible that this is the ministry of the Holy Spirit, I realize that my experience conforms to the teaching and testimony of Scripture. Changed lives are the most powerful testimony to the importance of the Bible.

The Bible speaks convincingly of life after death.

THINKING BACK

Why is the Bible so important? The Bible is, as we have seen, a massive historical presence. Its influence on nearly every area of life is difficult to exaggerate. Suffice it to say, the world would be a darker, uglier, crueler place than we can imagine if it were not for the light, beauty, and love revealed in the Bible.

SPEED BUMP!

Slow down to be sure you've gotten the main points of this section.

1. **What influence has the Bible had on our society?**
The Bible has played a major role in determining the social values of the Western world.

2. **What influence has the Bible had on our culture?**
The Bible has been a dominant influence in the arts of the Western world.

3. **What influence has the Bible had on our spiritual life?**
The Bible has been a dominant influence in the spiritual, moral, and ethical formation of the Western world.

FOR FURTHER STUDY

Scripture Passages

- Exodus 20:1-17
- Matthew 25:34-40
- Matthew 26:11
- Luke 6:31

- Romans 1:18-20
- 1 Corinthians 15:19
- 2 Corinthians 5:17
- James 2:8-9

Read these passages and consider how they add to your understanding of the information in this section.

FAQ #4

Does the Bible Contain Errors?

The Bible, as originally written, was without error.

If there were mistakes in the Bible, and the Bible is the word of God, then God would be the author of mistakes. If God is the author of mistakes, then He is not what the Bible claims He is. So if we are to rely on God, we must have a reliable Bible. We must have confidence that the Bible is a book without error.

Plainly stated, no error in biblical fact can be demonstrated. People often get the impression that errors or contradictions riddle the Bible, but everything that seems to be an error or contradiction can be explained. For example, Matthew only mentions one angel at the tomb after Jesus' resurrection (Matthew 28:1-8). Luke mentions two angels (Luke 24:4). This is not a contradiction, as some people claim. Wherever you have two angels, it is a mathematical necessity that you must have one angel. If Matthew had said there was only one angel, then there would have been a contradiction, but he did not. He merely mentioned the angel who said the words that Matthew recorded.

In a more complex example, the four Gospels differ in their account as to what was written on a sign that was nailed to the cross above Jesus' head when He was crucified. Matthew says, "This is Jesus, the king of the Jews." Mark says, "The king of the Jews." Luke says, "This is the

> If the Bible is not true religion, one is very excusable in being deceived, for everything in it is grand and worthy of God. The more I consider the Gospel, the more I am assured there is nothing there which is not beyond the march of events and above the human mind.
>
> *Napoleon Bonaparte*

king of the Jews," and John says, "Jesus of Nazareth the king of the Jews." True, all of these are different. However, none of these accounts say that this was all that was written on the sign. The whole thing can be reconciled by realizing that the sign contained everything that was written: "This is Jesus of Nazareth, the king of the Jews." From this full statement, each author, for reasons of his own, articulated only part of the statement, but there is no error.

The Bible expresses truth without error in the ways truth was expressed in ancient times.

I may tell my wife that I am going to the post office. When I get home, I tell her that I picked up a screwdriver at the hardware store. Did I lie to her by not telling her I was going to the hardware store? No. I did go to the post office, and I did not tell her that I was going only to the post office. I did not give her all the truth, but everything I gave her was true.

Many people who say the Bible is a book of mythology, or that it is filled with contradictions and riddled with errors haven't read or studied the Bible much. They have not analyzed the Bible sufficiently in its own ancient context to examine its credibility. People base their whole eternity on an off-the-cuff comment by some professor in college or an unsubstantiated allegation by some colleague at work. How unwise! When we respond to such allegations or to any biblical questions we may have, it is very important to remember two truths about the Bible: (1) God is true and faithful and never deceives or leads anyone astray, so we can trust that His word, given to us in the Bible, has the same qualities. (2) God's word was given through human authors who expressed it in the ways and manners that people of their times expressed truth. So modern readers must learn those ways and keep them in mind as they read the Bible. The Bible is without error. Any apparent error or contradiction can be credibly explained.

FAQ #5

 Are the Bible Manuscripts Reliable?

 The Bible that we have today says essentially the same thing as the original Bible.

Ancient copies of the Bible or portions of the Bible that were hand-copied before the invention of the printing press are called manuscripts. Although some discrepancies in the various ancient manuscripts exist, they are insignificant, and have no bearing on any doctrine. For example, some of the discrepancies are like the difference between spelling the word color as "c-o-l-o-r"—the way we do in America, or "c-o-l-o-u-r"—the British way of spelling it. There are also some discrepancies in numbers and words and occasional phrases. These variances are very few and affect no doctrine. According to Bruce Metzger, a New Testament scholar who taught at Princeton, after 2,000 years of being copied, only forty of the 20,000 lines in the New Testament are debatable today. Everything else is a given, and none of the variances affect the Christian faith.

Two other matters are important in establishing the reliability of the ancient manuscripts from which we get our English Bible: their number and their age. First, there are a ton of them. Conversely, only seven copies of Plato's *Tetralogies*, twenty copies of Caesar's *Gallic Wars*, and 643 copies of Homer's *Iliad* exist. But there are over 5,000 ancient manuscripts of the New Testament! That is remarkable, indeed! In addition to the New Testament documents, we have over 10,000 ancient manuscripts or parts of manu-

Evidence that the Bible has been preserved nearly perfectly for 2,000 years is greater than that available for any other book from ancient times.

scripts of the Old Testament. Of course, this multitude of manuscripts makes it easier to verify how accurately they have been copied and confirm what the original documents said. The Bible is easily the most common ancient document in existence, and by comparing this galaxy of manuscripts, we see that, aside from minute exceptions, they all say exactly the same thing. Our Bible today is reliable.

A second matter affecting the value of the manuscripts is their age. That is, how soon after the original was written were the copies made? In this regard, the New Testament manuscripts are again superior to other writings. For example, Caesar's *Gallic Wars* was written about 60 B.C., yet the earliest existing manuscript we have is dated A.D. 900, nearly 1,000 years later. Plato's *Tetralogies* was written in about 400 B.C., but the earliest manuscript dates to about A.D. 900, nearly 1,300 years later. And Homer's *Iliad* was written about 900 B.C., but the earliest copy we have dates to about 400 B.C., about 500 years later. The New Testament was completed no later than A.D. 100, yet the earliest known manuscript that contains most of the New Testament dates to about A.D. 200, a span of approximately 100 years. Some fragments date back as early as A.D. 125. Recently, a manuscript fragment of the New Testament was dated to before A.D. 100, during the lifetime of the apostle John, who was an author of parts of the New Testament.

One final piece of information enhances the credibility of the Bible manuscripts. Many people have heard of the Dead Sea Scrolls, but do not know why they are so important. These scrolls were found in 1947 in a series of caves in a desolate area just west of the Dead Sea. Between

Why I Need to Know This

The Bible claims to be the word of God. I need to know if it makes sense to believe this. Blind faith is not a sufficient platform on which to place one's eternal destiny. If I can reasonably justify accepting the Bible as the word of God, then I have a compass for life, giving me instruction in how to live on earth and assurance of life after death in heaven with God.

145 B.C. and A.D. 68, they were inhabited by a Jewish community protesting the leaders and practices they believed corrupted worship at the Jerusalem temple. For some reason, they stored a number of these scrolls in sealed jars, where they survived the ravages of time, so that many of them are readable today.

When found, the Dead Sea Scrolls were one thousand years older than the earliest previous Old Testament manuscript. By comparing the manuscripts, we know that, in one thousand years of copying, only one word in Isaiah 53—the word "light" in verse 11—differs from the earliest known manuscript found previously. This variation does not affect the meaning at all. So for all practical purposes, we know that the Old Testament manuscript remained unchanged from one thousand years earlier. This gives us great confidence in the reliability of Bible manuscripts.

In many cases, dedicated, scholarly monks or scribes copied these manuscripts. They viewed their task as a sacred labor of love. Some believed that a curse fell on anyone who added to or subtracted from the Scripture (Revelation 22:18-19). Therefore, they took exacting and painstaking measures to ensure accuracy. This explains why so few variations in manuscripts exist, and why we believe that the Bible we have today is, for all practical purposes, exactly the same as originally written.

FAQ #6

 How Does Archaeology Testify to the Accuracy of the Bible?

 Not one archaeological find disproves accounts in the Bible and many confirm the historical accuracy of the Bible.

Many of the attacks on the accuracy of the Bible began prior to modern archaeology. However, beginning with major excavations in the Holy Land in the mid-1800s, archaeological evidence has repeatedly confirmed the Bible's historical accuracy. As travel became easier and scholars more curious, archaeologists began to peel away the earth's surface to reveal ancient cities, painted tombs, solid gold likenesses of rulers, jars, money and items needed for the afterlife, tablets of stone and clay telling the story of a people or a city. As these artifacts emerged, references to biblical places and people surfaced. In a number of cases, people or places which skeptics had discussed as fanciful mistakes in the Bible were confirmed. In fact, many things that eighteenth- and nineteenth-century scholars questioned have now been verified as factual.

"**N**o archaeological discovery has ever controverted a biblical statement.

For example, Belshazzar, named in the Book of Daniel as the last king of Babylon, was nowhere to be found in Babylonian records. All known Babylonian records listed Nabonidus as the last king. Then, archaeological records revealed that during the time of Daniel, Nabonidus left Babylon for ten years and went to Arabia. In his absence, his son Belshazzar ruled as king. In this way, archaeology explained the apparent discrepancy between the biblical record and the previous Babylonian record (Paul Little, *Know Why You Believe*, p. 95).

Clifford Wilson, a committed Christian and retired archaeologist at the University of Sydney in Australia, found evidence of a man named Sanballat who lived during the time of Alexander the Great. A man named Sanballat is also found in the Book of Nehemiah, before Alexander the Great's time. Critics often cited this as proof of historical error in the Bible. But then it was discovered that there were three Sanballats, and that one of them lived during the time of Nehemiah. The Bible was correct after all ("The Bible: Fable, Fraud or Fact," Coral Ridge Video Ministry, January 4, 1994).

More than a century of biblical excavations at over 25,000 sites have repeatedly confirmed the accuracy of the Bible. After working in the field for many years, noted archaeologist Nelson Glueck said, "No archaeological discovery has ever controverted [contradicted] a single, properly understood Biblical statement." (quoted in Josh McDowell's *New Evidence that Demands a Verdict*, p. 370).

To be completely candid, we must assess what all this means. By itself, this does not mean that the Bible is the word of God. It does mean that the Bible has never been proven wrong on any point of history or geography. However, the historical-geographical test must be passed if we are to conclude that the Bible is the word of God. Since there are no mistakes, it passes the test and allows us, on that basis, to conclude that it is the word of God. Whether or not we decide it is the word of God is ultimately a matter of faith, but we would not be able to make that conclusion if we found the Bible riddled with error.

FAQ #7

 Does Fulfilled Prophecy Testify to the Identity of the Bible as the Word of God?

 The fulfilled prophecies of the Bible lend powerful support to its being the word of God.

The Bible is the only book in the world that has specific prophecies clearly fulfilled hundreds of years after they were given. Jesus fulfilled many Old Testament prophecies, some of them more obvious than others. For our purposes, we will focus on the more obvious ones. Let the record speak for itself.

1. Prophecy: **The Messiah would be born of a virgin.**
"**Therefore the L**ORD **Himself will give you a sign: Behold a virgin will be with child and bear a son, and she will call His name Immanuel" (Isaiah 7:14 NASB).**
Fulfillment: **Jesus was born of the virgin Mary. "She was found to be with child by the Holy Spirit. And Joseph... kept her a virgin until she gave birth to a Son; and he called His name Jesus" (Matthew 1:18-25 NASB).**

2. Prophecy: **The Messiah would be born into the family of King David. "Behold the days are coming, declares the L**ORD**, when I shall raise up for David a righteous Branch; and He will reign as king and act wisely and do justice and righteousness in the land" (Jeremiah 23:5 NASB).**
Fulfillment: **In the genealogy in the Gospel of Luke, Jesus is listed as being in the lineage of David. "Jesus... the son of David. " (Luke 3:23-31).**

3. Prophecy: **The Messiah would be born in the city of Bethlehem. "But as for you, Bethlehem... too little to be among the clans of Judah, from you One will go forth for Me to be ruler in Israel. His goings forth are from long ago, from the days of eternity" (Micah 5:2 NASB).**
Fulfillment: **Jesus was born in Bethlehem. "For today in the city of David (Bethlehem) there has been born for you a Savior, who is Christ the Lord" (Luke 2:11 NASB).**

These prophecies describe the birth of Jesus, the Messiah. Other remarkable prophecies from the Old Testament and Gospels describe His death.

4. Prophecy: **The Messiah would be betrayed by a friend. "Even my close friend, in whom I trusted, who ate my bread, has lifted up his heel against me" (Psalm 41:9 NASB).**
Fulfillment: **Jesus was betrayed by Judas Iscariot, one of His twelve disciples. "Judas Iscariot, who also betrayed Him" (Matthew 10:4).**

5. Prophecy: **The Messiah would be tortured and crucified. "But He was pierced through for our transgressions, He was crushed for our iniquities. The chastening for our well-being fell upon Him, and by His scourging we are healed" (Isaiah 53:5 NASB).**

Fulfillment: Jesus was beaten and then crucified. "Then he (Pilate) released Barabbas for them; but after having Jesus scourged, he delivered Him to be crucified" (Matthew 27:26 NASB).

6. **Prophecy: Jesus would rise from the dead. "For Thou wilt not abandon my soul to Sheol (the place of the departed dead); neither wilt Thou allow Thy Holy One to undergo decay" (Psalm 16:10 NASB).**
Fulfillment: Jesus rose from the dead. "And the angel answered and said to the women, "Do not be afraid; for I know that you are looking for Jesus who has been crucified. He is not here, for He has risen, just as He said. Come, see the place where He was lying" (Matthew 28:5-6 NASB).

There are many more prophecies and fulfillments. In McDowell's *New Evidence that Demands a Verdict*, (p. 193), we see that the odds of any man, past and present, fulfilling only eight of the major prophecies that Jesus fulfilled are 1 in 10 to the 17th power. That is, one in 100,000,000,000,000,000!

In order to help us comprehend these staggering odds, suppose we take this many silver dollars (10 to the 17th power) and lay them on the face of Texas. Now, as you know, Texas is a big state. If you could flip Texas west using El Paso as a hinge, Houston would land in the Pacific Ocean. If you could flip Texas east, using Houston as a hinge, El Paso would land in the Atlantic. If you could flip Texas north using the top of the panhandle as a hinge, the lowest part of Texas would land just short of the Canadian border. This many silver dollars (10 to the 17th power) would cover the entire state two feet deep in coins.

Now imagine that one of those silver dollars was painted red. Blindfold a man and tell him that he can travel anywhere in the state he wants to, and pick up one silver dollar. Keep in mind that traveling at seventy miles per hour, he could not drive across Texas in a day. His chances of getting the marked silver dollar are approximately the same

Jesus fulfilled all messianic prophecies.

as a person fulfilling eight major prophecies of the Messiah. Now, consider that Jesus fulfilled forty-eight prophecies. The odds that any one man fulfilled all forty-eight are 10 to the 157th power. There is no practical way even to illustrate that number. Let's just say that there is a better chance of a tornado going through a junk yard and perfectly assembling an automobile. When we look at the fulfilled prophecies in the life of Christ, the Bible becomes a very convincing book, and Jesus becomes a very convincing Messiah, God the Son.

Of course, these prophecies deal only with Jesus. But many more prophecies in the Bible were fulfilled. These are not fortune-cookie prophecies, like "an attractive person will soon come into your life," or "things will soon begin looking up for you." No, these are specific and verifiable. The Bible itself makes it clear that fulfilled prophecy attests to the supernatural origin of the word of its prophets (Jeremiah 28:9). If a prophet spoke anything that did not come true, he was not a true prophet (Deuteronomy 18:20-22) and was to be stoned.

The odds of these prophecies being accidentally fulfilled are virtually zero. But look at the record of the psychics in the tabloid papers. No one is able, on any level of credibility, to prophesy things that come true. Yet the Bible is full of such prophecies. They create a set of odds so remarkable that, if the prophecies are believed, they validate the Bible as the word of God. You dismiss them only if you do not want to accept that conclusion.

FAQ #8

Do Changed Lives Testify to the Truth of the Bible?

The hearts of millions of people over the last two thousand years have been transformed by the Bible, lending weight to its divine claim.

Today, the explosion of Christianity, especially in places where the governments have tried to illuminate it, is a phenomenon demanding explanation. What could account for it? From the first twelve disciples to today, many would benefit tremendously by denying Christianity, and yet they won't. Why? Because they cannot deny the most important thing in their lives. Most of the twelve disciples died a tortured death because of their faith. They really knew what was going on with Jesus' death, burial, resurrection, post-resurrection appearances, and His ascension. Would every one of them die a dreadful death for something he thought was a lie? They said, in essence, "Go ahead and kill me if you want to, but I know it is true." They had every reason to recant their position, but they didn't.

The odds of biblical prophecies being accidentally fulfilled are nearly zero.

Since the time of the apostles, thousands have followed in their footsteps. *Foxe's Book of Martyrs* presents an account of many early Christians who died for their faith. The stories send a deep chill into the bones of anyone who reads them. People were sawed in half, fed to wild animals, and forced to stand unprotected in the cold until they froze to death. They could have escaped this by denying Jesus, but they wouldn't do it.

If this happened only in random sects, as in the infamous Guyana Jonestown mass suicide of 1978, it would not be hard to explain. Many people have died in isolated instances for foolish causes. But this has been going on for two thousand years. Millions of people have said, in essence, "I believe the Bible to be the word of God because of the impact it has had on my life, and I am willing to die for it."

For one thing, the Bible is true to reality. For example, it commands us to be sexually pure and warns us of danger if we are not. "Flee immorality. Every other sin that a man commits is outside the body, but the immoral man sins against his own body" (1 Corinthians 6:18 NASB). When people disregard this commandment, sexually transmitted diseases such as AIDS, herpes, syphilis, and gonorrhea begin to ravage the body. When a person commits sexual sin, he sins against his own body.

The Bible commands husbands to love their wives just as Christ loved the church and gave Himself up for her. It also commands wives to respect their husbands (Ephesians 5:25, 33). In this way, a marriage will be preserved and flourish. If one or both spouses violate these commands, the relationship often deteriorates and is frequently destroyed.

The
Bible is true
reality.

The Bible commands the laborer to work as unto the Lord, for it is the Lord Jesus whom he serves (Colossians 3:23-24), and it commands employers to treat their employees well, knowing that the master of both employer and employee is in heaven (Ephesians 6:9). When this happens, labor relations are good, productivity is likely to be high, and the economy thrives. When these commands are disobeyed, the workplace erodes.

Hundreds, and perhaps thousands, of examples demonstrate the truth of the Bible. The Bible possesses wisdom and an understanding of the human spirit and of circumstances. By adhering to the teachings of the Bible, life can be aligned with principles that bring success; violating them can bring about failure. The Bible's truth also supports the claim that the Bible is the word of God.

Additionally, people's lives have been dramatically changed as a result of becoming a Christian and following the Bible. I am one of those people. I asked God to prove His reality to me somehow, and I repented of my sin and invited Christ into my life. I have been in a continual state of change ever since. No matter what price I have to pay, even if it's with my own life, I will never regret becoming a Christian. My testimony is only a whisper among a vast human chorus of testimonies accumulated over the last two thousand years. The Bible transformed my life, and I believe it to be the word of God.

THINKING BACK

A single strand of evidence does not prove the Bible is the word of God. But the weight of all of them taken together enables a person to believe that the Bible is the word of God. And the evidence is strong indeed.

SPEED BUMP!

1. **Does the Bible contain errors?**
The Bible, as originally written, was without error.

2. **Are the Bible manuscripts reliable?**
The Bible that we have today says essentially the same thing as the original Bible.

3. **How does archaeology testify to the accuracy of the Bible?**
Not one archaeological find disproves accounts in the Bible and many confirm the historical accuracy of the Bible.

4. **Does fulfilled prophecy testify to the identity of the Bible as the word of God?**
The fulfilled prophecies of the Bible lend powerful support to its being the word of God.

5. **Do changed lives testify to the truth of the Bible?**
The hearts of millions of people over the last two thousand years have been transformed by the Bible, lending weight to its divine claim.

FOR FURTHER STUDY

Scripture Passages

- Matthew 4:1-11
- Matthew 5:18
- Luke 24:25-27
- John 10:35
- 2 Peter 3:16

FAQ #9

 How Did God Communicate His Truth to Us?

 Through several channels, God revealed to us the information He wanted us to know.

The Bible is an amazing book. It was written:

- over a period of 1,500 years
- by over forty different authors ranging from farmers to kings
- in mainly two different languages
- in many different countries
- about hundreds of different subjects.

Despite these overwhelming facts, it manifests a unity that could exist only if one author were responsible for its contents. The author of the Bible is God, who has revealed His message to humanity.

The process of God's communicating reliably to humanity involves four different aspects. Revelation has to do with God unveiling Himself and truth to humanity. Inspiration deals with God overseeing the process of recording His revelation without error. Illumination refers to the ministry of the Holy Spirit that enables believers to properly understand Scripture. Canonicity refers to the process

> I have always believed in the inspiration of the Holy Scriptures whereby they have become the expression to man of the Word and will of God. No book of any kind ever written has ever so affected the whole of life of a people.
>
> *President Warren G. Harding*

of recognizing and collecting Scripture. In these pages, we examine the process of revelation.

To reveal means to "unveil." Revelation has often been defined as "God's making known to humanity that which would otherwise be unknown." However, the concept is really a little more complex. That definition must be understood in light of the fact that there are two different kinds of revelation. One is called general revelation and the other, specific or special revelation.

General Revelation

General revelation refers to all revelation from God apart from Christ and the Bible. That would include several things:

1. **Nature. Who has not looked up into the night sky with stars glittering like so many tiny crystals on black velvet, and thought "There must be a God!" That is no accident. God intended for creation to reflect Him as any piece of art reflects the artist and draws the onlooker's mind from the creation to the creator. The beauty, order, magnitude, and intricacy of nature reveal to us that there is a God (Romans 1:18-20).**

2. **Providence. God's intervention into the affairs of people often gives evidence of His existence. For instance, more than one person who served in Vietnam acknowledges that they should have died there, but almost miraculously didn't. As a result, they expressed a feeling that God has spared them for some reason. In dealing with nations, God has done things to cause some nations to rise and others to fall, which gives rise to speculation about divine intervention. There are any number of fairly small things which, if they had gone differently, would have resulted in the United States' losing the Revolutionary War against England. Because those things benefited our side, and because one result of the victory has been the unparalleled Christian influence of the United States**

on the world, we have become aware of God's providence in our national affairs (Romans 8:28).

3. Conscience. Something deep inside people inclines them to believe in the divinely supernatural. This inner conscience speaks of the existence of God to all of us. King Solomon described it when he said "[God] has put eternity in their (humanity's) hearts" (Ecclesiastes 3:11). Humanity's moral nature and its inner sense of right and wrong are part of this conscience. Although cultures differ in the acts each deem right and wrong, all cultures have a sense of right and wrong. In all cultures, no matter how primitive, a person can "violate his own conscience." Explaining this phenomenon turns our thoughts to God, since God accounts for the fact that all people possess conscience (Genesis 1:27).

The written word transmits the revelation of the Living Word.

Nature, providence, conscience, and the moral nature of humankind all point us to God, and constitute general revelation. This general revelation is sufficient to plant the existence of God and the concept of right and wrong in our minds, and to draw our minds toward God.

Special Revelation

Special revelation refers to revelation that has come to us through the Bible and the life of Jesus.

1. Bible. Without the Bible, we might believe in the existence of God, but we would not know who He is, what He is like, if He wants or expects anything from us, or how to get to know Him. The Bible fills in those gaps. Through the

Scripture, we can understand who God is and how to develop a relationship with Him.

2. Jesus. The Bible calls Jesus the Word of God (John 1:1; Revelation 19:13), which reveals a very close connection in the mind of God the Father, between the written word (the Bible) and the Living Word (Jesus). Jesus has fully revealed to us what God is like, how we can be related to Him, and what God expects of us. The Bible, God's written revelation, secures the revelation Jesus provided and transmits it to the extent that any writing can to all believers who lived after Jesus' earthly life. General revelation tells us that God exists, but only special revelation is sufficient to save us (Acts 4:12).

In summary, we can say that God has given each person on earth enough light to know which direction leads toward God. If a person turns away from God, he will never find Him. If a person walks toward God, he will eventually find Him. But in finding God, he learns that it was actually God who drew him. As C. S. Lewis so aptly stated, our saying that we found God is like the mouse saying it found the cat.

FAQ #10

How Did Fallible Men Record an Infallible Message?

God supernaturally inspired the writing of the Scriptures so that the writer, in his own personality, composed and recorded, without error, God's revelation in the original manuscripts or letters.

Inspiration

When we bring up the question of the infallibility of the Bible we are opening the subject of "inspiration." This word is easily misunderstood when applied to the Bible. We commonly speak of artists having been inspired to do great work. Shakespeare was inspired when he wrote *Hamlet*. An inspired Beethoven penned his Fifth Symphony. Michelangelo was inspired when he painted the Sistine Chapel. Sir Laurence Olivier gave an inspired performance of Richard III. Luciano Pavarotti sang an inspired role in Puccini's *La Boheme*. By these uses of "inspired" we mean, simply, that they transcend the ordinary. The individual reached down within himself and produced a work that was extraordinary even for other geniuses, or even for himself.

"Inspiration" applied to the Bible means that all Scripture originates from God.

This is not what is meant when we say the Bible is inspired. The word "inspired," when it is used in reference to the Bible, is a technical term meaning "God-breathed." In 2 Timothy 3:16 we read, "All Scripture is given by inspiration of God [literally, is God-breathed], and is profitable for doctrine, for reproof, for correction, for instruction in righteousness, that the man of God may be complete, thoroughly equipped for every good work."

Another key passage in understanding inspiration is 2 Peter 1:20-21, which says, "No prophecy of Scripture is of any private interpretation, for prophecy never came by the will of man, but holy men of God spoke as they were moved by the Holy Spirit."

These two passages together picture Scripture as coming to us from God through men. But these men were not writing purely human documents. They were being supernaturally guided to write what God wanted written, although no evidence suggests that they were taking dictation from God. Each man's own personality, background, writing style, and temperament are revealed. You can tell when you are reading John instead of Paul, for example. Once you get to know their styles, they are easily identifiable. Jeremiah did not write like Isaiah. God worked through human agents so that, using their own individual characteristics, they composed and recorded without error God's revelation to humanity in the words of the original manuscripts or letters.

Other Scriptures also claim divine origin. For example, in the Old

Testament, people commonly claimed to speak for God. In 2 Samuel 23:2-3, King David, as he lay dying said, "The Spirit of the LORD spoke by me, and His word was on my tongue. The God of Israel said, The Rock of Israel spoke to me: 'He who rules over men must be just, Ruling in the fear of God.'" The prophet Jeremiah said, "Then the LORD put forth His hand and touched my mouth, and the LORD said to me: 'Behold I have put My words in your mouth'" (Jeremiah 1:9-10).

When New Testament writers refer to portions of the Old Testament, they uniformly treat Scripture as nothing less than God's word. And one key text in the New Testament, 2 Peter 3:16, identifies Paul's writings, which were later gathered into our New Testament, as Scripture. Peter says that Paul's epistles contain "some things hard to understand, which untaught and unstable people twist to their own destruction, as they do also the rest of the Scriptures." Thus, wherever one part of our Bible refers to another, the reference either identifies that portion as Scripture, or God's word, or the reference uses the other portion in a manner fully consistent with the teaching of 2 Timothy 3:16.

Inerrancy

Not everyone understands the same thing when we say that God's word is inspired and without error. Some say that the Bible contains God's word, but that the Bible has error in it, and the parts that have error are not God's word. This presents a mountain too high to climb. Someone would have to decide which parts of the Bible have errors and which do not. Years ago, W. A. Criswell, former pastor of First Baptist Church of Dallas, Texas, summarized this theory: The Bible is inspired in spots and we're inspired to pick out the

Why I Need to Know This

I need to have confidence in the accuracy of the Bible and respect for the authority of the Bible. I need to understand that the Bible is not merely a work of humans, but a work of God, and that I need God's help to understand it.

spots. I agree with his conclusion that this is unacceptable. I don't trust myself to make those decisions, let alone anyone else. When you start saying that some parts of the Bible are inspired by God and therefore without error, but other parts have error and are therefore not inspired, you step onto a slippery slope. No two people are going to agree on which parts are inspired and inerrant and which parts aren't. You end up jeopardizing the Bible altogether. It is like letting a snake get its head through a hole. If it can get its head through, the rest of the snake can get through, as well.

Therefore, we have to arrive at a definition that is airtight. The Bible is verbally and totally inspired and without error in the original writings. All of the individual words, not just the concepts, are inspired and without error. All Scripture originates from God, who is true and faithful and fully capable of communicating truth without error to human writers. We have multiple testimony to assure us of this truth: the testimony of Scripture about itself, which we have just discussed; the testimony of the Holy Spirit dwelling within every true believer; the testimony of countless believers who have relied upon Scripture for guidance and salvation; and the testimony of devout and careful Bible scholars who have studied Scripture and have refuted the claims that Scripture contains error. Among such scholars, the testimony of Berkeley and Alvera M. Mickelsen is typical:

After examining thousands of passages of Scripture, [we] have concluded that the Bible teaches truth on all subjects it address-es in the ways and manners of expressing truth in ancient times. The Scriptures also illustrate truth by showing that error (idola-try, deceit, falsehood, and all forms of moral evil) brings tragedy (*Understanding Scripture*, p. 28).

Together these testimonies assure us that the Bible, as God's writ-ten word, is nothing less than pure truth.

FAQ #11

 How Can Humans Understand Divine Information?

 The Holy Spirit illumines the mind of the obedient believer to understand the spiritual truth of the Scripture.

Illumination

Several passages of Scripture help us arrive at our understanding of the illumining ministry of the Holy Spirit. John 16:12-15 says:

I have many more things to say to you, but you cannot bear them now. But when He, the Spirit of truth, comes, He will guide you into all the truth; for He will not speak on His own initiative, but whatever He hears, He will speak; and He will disclose to you what is to come. He shall glorify Me; for He shall take of Mine, and shall disclose it to you. All things that the Father has are Mine; therefore I said, that He takes of Mine, and will disclose it to you (NASB).

We add to Jesus' words the writings of the apostle Paul in 1 Corinthians 2:9-3:3:

As it is written, "things which eye has not seen and ear has not heard, and which have not entered the heart of man, all that God has prepared for those who love him." For to us God revealed them through the Spirit; for the Spirit searches all things, even the depths of God. For who among men knows the thoughts of a man except the spirit of the man, which is in him? Even so the thoughts of God no one knows except the Spirit of God.

Now we have received, not the spirit of the world, but the Spirit who is from God, that we might know the things freely given to us by God, which things we also speak, not in words taught by human wisdom, but in those taught by the Spirit, combining spiritual thoughts with spiritual words. But a natural man does not accept the things of the Spirit of God; for they are foolishness to him, and he cannot understand them, because they are spiritually appraised.

But he who is spiritual appraises all things, yet he himself is appraised by no man. For who has known the mind of the Lord, that he should instruct him? But we have the mind of Christ. And I, brethren, could not speak to you as to spiritual men, but as to men of flesh, as to babes in Christ. I gave you milk to drink, not solid food; for you were not yet able to receive it. Indeed, even now you are not yet able, for you are still fleshly (NASB).

Finally, we read the words of the apostle John:

And as for you, the anointing which you received from Him abides in you, and you have no need for anyone to teach you; but as His anointing teaches you about all things, and is true and is not a lie, and just as it has taught you, you abide in Him (1 John 2:27).

From these passages, we learn several things:

1. The Holy Spirit helps Christians understand the spiritual things of the Bible.

2. The more spiritually mature a Christian is, the more he can understand.

3. Nothing can substitute for this ministry. The truth may be grasped only by the illuminating ministry of the Spirit.

Certainly, the "natural man," the non-Christian, can understand some things of the Bible. For example, when it says that Jesus walked from Bethany to Jerusalem, the natural man is capable of understanding that. The spiritual truths—what Paul called "the things freely given to us by God...those [words] taught by the Spirit, combining spiritual {thoughts} with spiritual words"—can only be understood by Christians.

FAQ #12

 How Was the Bible Finally Compiled?

 The church's recognition of books and letters that were inspired by God and collected in the Bible was sovereignly governed by Him.

Canonicity

If the Bible did not come to us in a completed package from a cloud-topped mountain, where did the actual book come from? How did we get it? How did we get what is called the "canon?" (Canon means "accepted as genuine writings.") How was it determined what books were accepted as Scripture and included in the Bible? These questions must be answered for the Old Testament first, and then the New Testament.

Old Testament Canon

First, an important point must be made. A letter or manuscript belonged in the Old Testament canon if it was inspired by God. But how was it decided whether or not a given letter or manuscript was inspired by God? That question is the same for both the Old and New Testaments, but the answers are somewhat different. For the Old Testament, it is not clear to us on what grounds the authority of a writing was accepted. That it was accepted, however, is clear. Jesus Himself stamped His approval on the thirty-nine books which make up our Old Testament. In Luke 11:51, Jesus rebukes the hypocritical religious leaders of His time. He was pronouncing a series of "woes" on them for their attitudes and actions. "Woe to you Pharisees! For you love the best seats in the synagogues and greetings in the marketplaces. Woe to you, scribes and Pharisees, hypocrites! For you are like graves which are not seen, and the men who walk over them are not aware of them!"

Jesus stamped His approval on the thirty-nine books that make up our Old Testament.

He pronounced one "woe" on them because they had shed the blood of the prophets "from the blood of Abel to the blood of Zechariah." This statement makes sense when we understand how the Hebrew Bible and the Old Testament of our English Bible are organized differently. In the Hebrew Bible, Genesis is the first book and 2 Chronicles, instead of Malachi, is the last. Abel is found in the first book of the Hebrew Bible, Genesis. Zechariah is found in the last book of the Hebrew Bible, 2 Chronicles. When Jesus blasts them for shedding the blood of the first prophet to the last prophet and all prophets in between, He is really saying, "Your guilt is recorded through the entire Bible, from Genesis to 2 Chronicles!"

Some people claim that all the books of the Old Testament canon were recognized and collected into one volume by Ezra in the fifth century B.C. References by the Jewish historian Josephus, whose life overlapped that of the apostles, indicate that the thirty-nine books which we recognize today as the Old Testament were recognized as Scripture then.

Other facts support this conclusion, giving us good reason to believe that all the books of our Old Testament were accepted by devout Jews as Scripture by the time of Jesus.

New Testament Canon

How the New Testament books were recognized and collected into one volume is somewhat clearer. Again, we restate that books were Scripture because they were inspired by God. However, God did not give us a list of the inspired books to be collected into the New Testament. In His sovereignty, He oversaw that process from heaven.

Many of the New Testament books were written by the apostles. Paul and Peter clearly wrote with their apostolic authority in mind. Peter specifically refers to Paul's letters as Scripture:

Our beloved brother Paul, according to the wisdom given to him, has written to you, as also in all his [letters], speaking in them of these things, in which are some things hard to understand, which untaught and unstable people twist to their own destruction, as they do also the rest of the Scriptures (2 Peter 3:15-16).

One criterion of inspiration was whether or not the document was written by an apostle. Although not apostles, Mark and Luke carried great weight because they were such close associates of the apostles. A second criterion was whether or not they were recognized as authoritative by the early church. This criterion is important because, as books were written during the lifetime of the apostles, the apostles could easily have aided in the process of recognizing inspired writings. Once

Although God inspired each New Testament book, He did not give us a list of the books to be included.

their approval was given to a letter or book, that approval was passed down through church tradition. A third criterion was whether or not the letter or book conformed to the high standards set by other books that were already recognized as Scripture.

The result of this process was that the books we have in our Old and New Testaments were officially acknowledged as Scripture by the Council of Carthage, a gathering of church leaders in A.D. 397, around three hundred years after the death of the last apostle, John. Since that time, the thirty-nine Old Testament books and the twenty-seven New Testament books have formed the canon of Scripture for all Christians—a list that, for Protestant believers, remains unchanged today.

While it is interesting and helpful to know about the formation of the canon of Scriptural books and letters, we must rest on the sovereignty of God for their authenticity. If God is going to hold us accountable to truth, He must see to it that we have the truth. God, in His providence, governed the process of forming the canon. The witness of the Spirit in the hearts of believers who read the Scriptures, and the change which the Holy Spirit brings about in their lives, is the final telling testimony to the fact that we have the Word of God as He intended.

SPEED BUMP!

1. **How did God communicate His truth to us?**
Through several channels, God revealed to us the information He wanted us to know.

2. **How did fallible men record an infallible message?**
God supernaturally inspired the writing of the Scriptures so that the writer, in his own personality, composed and recorded, without error, God's revelation in the original manuscripts or letters.

3. **How can humans understand divine information?**
The Holy Spirit illumines the mind of the obedient believer to understand the spiritual truth of the Scripture.

4. **How was the Bible finally compiled?**

The church's recognition of books and letters that were inspired by God and collected in the Bible was sovereignly governed by Him.

FOR FURTHER STUDY

Scripture Passages

- Matthew 5:18
- Hebrews 4:12
- Luke 24:25-27
- 2 Peter 1:21
- 1 Timothy 3:16
- 2 Peter 3:15-16

FAQ #13

 How Has the Bible Been Viewed by Those Who Reject Christianity?

 Some view the Bible solely as a product of human insight, and reject it as being the word of God.

Actually, three main groups of people fill this category. First there are atheists. They believe that they know enough to claim that there is no God. Ironically, no one could know that for sure unless he were omniscient (all-knowing), which is a supernatural ability. Would the atheist

> I have but this to say, the Bible is the best gift God has given to man. All the good the Savior gave to the world was communicated through this book. But for it we could not know right from wrong. All things most desirable for man's welfare, here and hereafter, are to be found portrayed in it.
>
> *Abraham Lincoln*

then be god? That logical inconsistency aside, atheists believe that the Bible is a book of human insight, wisdom, and experience, but is no more divine in origin than Shakespeare, Plato, or Socrates. They consider the evidence supporting the divine origin of Scripture untrustworthy or inconclusive. Atheists will admit that a great deal of practical wisdom can be found in the Bible, and that by following it, life on earth can be improved (such as doing unto others as you would have others do unto you—the Golden Rule). Beyond that, the book holds no credibility for them. Fulfilled prophecies are fabrications or coincidences. Divine claims are worthless, since anyone can claim divine authority. The resurrection is a hoax or a mystery, and not capable of lending credibility to Scripture. This is no surprise, of course. What else would we expect of atheists? Those who accept the message of the Bible cannot be atheists.

The second group of people, agnostics, say that they don't know if the Bible is the word of God. They stop short of saying that it isn't. They say it is not possible to know, or at least not possible for them to know, if the Bible is the word of God. However, rather than to err on the side of safety, agnostics fall short of treating it as a divine document.

Unlike the atheist and agnostic, the third kind of person who rejects Christianity has adopted a religion based on another body of religious writing. For example, a Muslim has his own religious book, the Koran, which cannot be true if the Bible is true. The books contradict each other. For example, since the prophet Muhammad, the founder of Islam, was not born until A.D. 570, Muslims consider Abraham, Jonah, Moses, and Jesus to be prophets of God, and all their writings as scripture until the final revelation (the Koran) of the last prophet, Muhammad. Anyone who does not accept the teachings of the Koran as the final authority merely proves that he is not a sincere follower of Allah (God). Therefore, Jesus was merely a prophet, and not to be followed as the ultimate authority. Jesus made a similar claim years before Muhammad ever came on the scene. He said, "I am the way, the truth and the life. No one comes to the Father except through Me" (John 14:6).

Similar circumstances exist with all other established and organized religions. If you are a Buddhist, a Hindu or a Confucianist, you cannot be a Christian. Therefore, followers of other religions, as well as agnostics and atheists, do not view the Bible as the exclusive, authoritative word of God.

FAQ #14

 How Has the Bible Been Viewed by Those Who Think That Part, but not All, of the Bible Is the Word of God?

 Some people believe that, while not all the Bible is the word of God, the Bible contains the word of God.

Two camps of people believe that the Bible may not be entirely the word of God, but that it contains the word of God. Those in the first camp have studied or been influenced by what is called "higher criticism" or the "historical-critical" method. They do not believe in the miraculous power of God. This discipline goes back about two hundred years to Germany, where scholars began their study of the Bible without assuming it was different from any other literature. The leader seems to have been a professor, Johann Salomo Semler, who taught at the University of Halle. Harold Lindsell, in his book, *God's Incomparable Word*, outlines the historical development of this line of thought. Apparently, Semler did not believe in the divine inspiration of the Bible. He rejected miracles and the supernatural in general. Therefore, anything in the Bible that included miracles and the

The most important question about the Bible is, Do you believe God has communicated to us in a reliable way?

supernatural had to be explained. He explained them by saying that matters relating to faith were the word of God, but matters relating to history or science were not the word of God, and filled with errors. As Semler would have put it, the Bible is not the word of God, but it contains the word of God.

Therefore, the task of many scholars for the last two hundred years has been to find the word of God within the Bible. This poses an impossibility, however, because no two people agree on what is the word of God and what are merely the writings of men. No two modern critics have ever provided exactly the same answers as to what is the word of God. Each person must discover the word of God for himself as he reads. As a result, preachers cannot preach the Bible as the authoritative word of God. They cannot say, "God says," because someone in the congregation can say, "well, you may think God said that, but I don't think He did! And why should I accept your conclusions if I don't agree with you?"

At its heart, it is a philosophical and theological problem. By that I mean that you cannot prove your point no matter what position you take. If you say all the Bible is the word of God, or if you say that only part of the Bible is the word of God, you cannot prove your position. The question is, do you believe that God has communicated to us in a reliable way or not? Do you believe that God performs miracles or not? (What good is a God if He cannot perform miracles?) Do you believe that God would leave us to our own ability to "reason out" what is the word of God and what is not? Humanity's unnotable ability to reason should give anyone pause to doubt.

Matters of history and of faith are so intertwined that they can't be separated.

Life becomes subjective guesswork unless all the Bible is the word of God. Recently, a group of seventy scholars got together and voted on what part of the Gospels were said by Jesus, and what parts were added by writers who attributed to Jesus things He did not really say. We are reduced to voting, or just deciding on our own, what is the word of God and what isn't.

Several specific problems are worth noting. First, as has been shown, the Bible becomes a subjective book, vulnerable to the whims of whomever reads it.

Historical-critical thinkers hold to the position that the Bible contains errors in the areas of history and science, but that it is accurate in matters of faith and practice. The problem is that matters of history and science are often intertwined with matters of faith and practice. Take the Resurrection, for example. History and science would tell you that the Resurrection could not have happened. But the Bible says that it did. Jesus said that it did. His disciples said that it did. We are exhorted to live in hope that when we die, we will be resurrected just as Jesus was. We are encouraged to take strength in this life, knowing that in the next life we will be delivered from all pain, suffering, and sorrow. If Jesus didn't rise from the dead, we can take no hope in such things. We cannot draw strength from them. We have no reason to follow Jesus' example in suffering. Paul said that if the resurrection is not true then our faith is in vain, the apostles are liars, and we are to be pitied above all other people (1 Corinthians 15:14-19). History and faith issues are so interwoven that we cannot separate them. The whole fabric becomes unraveled when we start pulling threads.

Ethics also collapse. If Paul is wrong in a given ethical teaching, as some modern scholars claim he is, why is he not wrong on other ethical teachings? You cannot use the words right and wrong anymore, because no one can say authoritatively what is right and what is wrong. Too much of the foundation for determining right and wrong from the Scripture has eroded. We fall into situational ethics, subjectivity reigns supreme, and any basis for objectivity is lost.

Lindsell writes:

Years ago, Bishop G. Bromley Oxnam of the Methodist Church said that God never ordered the slaughter of the Midianites and any God who did this is a "Dirty Bully." Yet the Scripture says God did just that, and claims that God is holy, just and righteous.

Still others say that God did not and could not have ordered Abraham to offer up Isaac as a burnt offering on Mt. Moriah. What does all of this mean?

> In every case, it means that people who hold these views reject what the Scriptures assert. They do it, not on the basis of Scripture, but on the basis of so-called evidence outside the Scripture that is used to judge Scripture. Or they do it because it is their subjective opinion that what happened is not credible. Now if what these critics assert is true, then at least these parts of the Bible are untrue. And what is untrue cannot be the word of God *(God's Incomparable Word,* p. 91).

When Scripture contradicts Scripture, then the Bible, as the word of God, has been destroyed, and subjectivity is the only principle of decision-making.

The second camp that believes the Bible may not be the word of God, but that it contains the word of God, are people who believe that all truth is relative. Philosophical kissing cousins of the historical-criticalists, they say, "Since all truth is relative, what may be true for you may not be true for me. But if it is true for you, go for it." These people would not challenge anyone who claimed to find truth in the Bible. They would just say, "Don't try to force your truth on us." Under these circumstances, these "relativists" would never agree that the whole Bible is the word of God, because then they would fall under the condemnation of God for not accepting Jesus.

FAQ #15

How Has the Bible Been Viewed by Those Who Accept Christianity and the Bible as the Word of God?

Although portions of the Bible have been contested at times, all Christians have historically agreed on a large body of truth.

If we say that we believe the Scriptures to be inspired, authoritative, and trustworthy, it would be odd indeed if we found that no one throughout the centuries held this view. Why should we believe it if no one else has, especially those who lived close to the time of the writing of the Scriptures? But if the church throughout history believed the Bible to be inspired, authoritative, and trustworthy, then that belief would be yet another pillar of support for the Bible. Our task, then, is to consider how the church, from earliest times to the present, has regarded the Bible.

The Old Testament scholars of Jesus' day, as well as Jesus, held the highest view of the Old Testament. Jesus said:

Do not think that I came to abolish the Law or the Prophets; I did not come to abolish, but to fulfill. For truly I say to you, until heaven and earth pass away, not the smallest letter or stroke shall pass away from the Law, until all is accomplished. Whoever then annuls one of the least of these commandments, and so teaches others, shall be called least in the kingdom of heaven; but whoever keeps and teaches them, he shall be called great in the kingdom of heaven (Matthew 5:17-19 NASB).

Never in any of Jesus' dealings with religious leaders did anyone question the authority and integrity of the Old Testament. Throughout the Bible, it is taken for granted that the Scriptures are the work of divine inspiration, and therefore inerrant, authoritative, and infallible. We read in Luke 22:37 the Scripture must be "accomplished". It was "written for our instruction," we read in Romans 15:4 and 1 Corinthians 10:11. Neither Jesus, nor a religious leader of His time, nor a New Testament writer would ever dream of questioning a statement contained in the Old Testament, although the exact manner or mode of its inspiration was not explained in the Old Testament. In the New Testament, Paul

Throughout history, the church has uniformly claimed the Bible's total truthfulness.

clearly stated in 2 Timothy 3:16-17, that "all Scripture is inspired by God and profitable for teaching, for reproof, for correction, for training in righteousness; that the man of God may be adequate, equipped for every good work" (NASB). This surely applied, in Paul's mind, to the Old Testament Scriptures, but may also have applied to New Testament Scripture, since the apostles seemed to be aware that things were being written in their day that were to be considered Scripture (2 Peter 3:16).

Not until the historical-critical method emerged from Europe about two hundred years ago did anyone question the inspiration, inerrancy, infallibility, and authority of Scripture. Until that time, the Scriptures were regarded as writings of the Holy Spirit, with no room left for the possibility that human hands might have corrupted the intention of God. The historic view is that the writers were used by God as a workman uses his tools; the actual words, rather than the writers, were considered inspired. All of the early orthodox church fathers reflected this viewpoint. Augustine, one of the greatest of the church fathers, and one who had a tremendous influence on Calvin, wrote, "The Faith will totter if the authority of the Holy Scriptures loses its hold on men. We must surrender ourselves to the authority of the Holy Scripture, for it can neither mislead nor be misled." He went on to say that once you admit a single error in the Bible, you open the door to a floodtide of disbelief. Disastrous consequences must follow the belief that anything false is found in the sacred books that the men by whom the Scripture has been given to us put down anything else in these books. It is one thing for a good man to deceive. But it's an entirely different matter for a writer of the Holy Scripture to deceive.

Augustine denied that anything false is found in Scripture.

Martin Luther, the leader of the Reformation in the 1500s, wrote, "This I have learned to do: to hold only those books which are called the Holy Scriptures in such honor that I finally believe that not one of the holy writers ever erred." This has been the historic position of the Catholic Church as well (Lindsell, p. 58).

Finally, we turn our attention to the witness of the various denominations and theological persuasions regarding the trustworthiness of the Bible. An excellent summary of these witnesses is found in Lindsell's book, and I draw upon his fine work to summarize some well-known positions.

The Westminster Confession of Faith. In Chapter One this confession, championed most conspicuously by Presbyterians, calls the Scripture the "only infallible rule of faith and practice."

Historic confessions affirm the complete inspiration and truthfulness of Scripture.

The Belgic Confession. This confession is advocated by the Reformed Church in America. In article 4 of the confession, we read:

We receive these books (the sixty-six books of the Old and New Testament), and only these books as holy and canonical, for the regulation, foundation, and confirmation of our faith; believing without any doubt all things contained in them, not so much because the Church receives and approves them as such, but more especially because the Holy Ghost witnesseth in our hearts that they are from God, whereof they carry the evidence

Why I Need to Know This

If I don't know this, I may be led astray by those who don't believe what the Bible says. I can rest in the fact that, while many true Christians disagree about certain areas of the Bible, there is, nevertheless, a larger body of information about which all Christians agree, and this contains information crucial to the Bible.

in themselves. For the very blind are able to perceive that the things foretold in them are fulfilling.

The New Hampshire Confession. This is Baptist-affiliated:

We believe that the Holy Bible was written by men divinely inspired, and is a perfect treasure of heavenly instruction: that it has God for its author, salvation for its end, and truth, without any mixture of error, for its matter; that it reveals the principles by which God will judge us; and therefore is, and shall remain to the end of the world, the true center of Christian union, and the supreme standard by which all human conduct, creeds, and opinions should be tried.

Lutheran Confessions. All the historic Lutheran confessions testify to the inspired, inerrant, infallible trustworthiness of the Bible.

Anglicans, Methodists, and Episcopalians. Although great diversity among these traditions exists today, the founding documents of these denominations include clear statements of belief in the inspiration, inerrancy, infallibility, and trustworthiness of the Bible.

There are devout and learned Christians who would wholeheartedly affirm the Bible's trustworthiness but would not affirm inerrancy as I have qualified it here. I do not want to question their spiritual integrity; however, when I look not only at the evidence, but also at the impossible situation that is created when humans have to decide what is the word of God and what is not, I deem it necessary to take a strict view of the subject. In the end, a person gives up the possibility of knowing anything for sure if he gives up on the inerrancy of the Bible.

When I look at the facts, it would take a courageous act for me to question not only scriptural statements, but also the church traditions that have existed from its inception. I believe the Bible is the word of God. The original writings do not err in matters spiritual, historical, or scientific. They teach truth on all subjects they address, in the ways and manners of expressing truth in ancient times. The Bible is God's revealed word to humankind for salvation and spiritual life.

SPEED BUMP!

1. How has the Bible been viewed by those who reject Christianity?
Some view the Bible solely as a product of human insight, and reject it as being the word of God.

2. How has the Bible been viewed by those who think that part, but not all, of the Bible is the word of God?
Some people believe that, while not all the Bible is the word of God, the Bible contains the word of God.

3. How has the Bible been viewed by those who accept Christianity and the Bible as the word of God?
Although portions of the Bible have been contested at times, all Christians have historically agreed on a large body of truth.

FOR FURTHER STUDY

Scripture Passages

- Matthew 5:17-19
- Revelation 22:18-19
- 2 Timothy 3:16-17
- 2 Peter 1:19-21

FAQ #16

 What Is the Capsule Summary of the Old Testament?

 The Old Testament is primarily the story of God's dealings with humanity through the nation of Israel.

The most basic storyline of the Old Testament is fairly simple. God created Adam and Eve, who sinned and were driven out of the Garden of Eden. As their offspring multiplied into the millions, sin also multiplied. Humanity became so sinful that God destroyed the earth with a universal flood, preserving Noah to repopulate the earth with a righteous family. Sin kept its grip on humanity, however, and once again people forgot God.

Many years later, God revealed Himself to Abraham and promised him a nation, many descendants, and a blessing that would extend to everyone on the earth. In believing God, Abraham became the father of a great people, the Hebrews, who were later known as the Jews. God's promises to Abraham were passed down through Isaac, Abraham's son, and Jacob, Abraham's grandson, and all twelve of Jacob's sons. From the twelve sons of Jacob descended the twelve tribes of Israel, who make up the Hebrew people.

A famine hit the land of Canaan (the same area, approximately, as the modern nation of Israel) where the Israelites were living, and they moved to Egypt for food. In time, they became a threat to the Egyptian people because they multiplied so rapidly, so the Egyptians enslaved the Hebrew people for nearly four hundred years. Finally, in response to their cries for

> Hammer away, ye hostile hands, your hammers break; God's anvil stands.
>
> *inscription on a monument to the Huguenots at Paris*

deliverance from slavery, God raised up Moses to lead them out of Egypt and back to the promised land of Canaan.

The Israelites, as they were then called, lived in the promised land in a loose governmental system for four hundred years. Then a monarchy was established, and numerous kings ruled the Hebrews for the next four hundred years. During the first one hundred twenty years of the monarchy, three famous kings reigned forty years each: Saul, David, and Solomon. Then as a result of civil conflict over taxation, the northern part of the nation seceded from the monarchy and established their own independent kingdom, called Israel. The southern kingdom adopted the name Judah.

After almost two hundred years, Assyria, a nation to the northeast, came and conquered the northern kingdom, Israel, and scattered many of them to the far corners of that part of the world. About one hundred years later, Babylonia invaded and conquered Assyria, as well as the southern kingdom of Judah, destroying Jerusalem and leading thousands of people into captivity in Babylonia.

About seventy years later, Persia defeated Babylonia to rule the part of the world from the eastern shore of the Mediterranean to India. The king of Persia allowed the Israelites, living in captivity in Babylonia, to return to Jerusalem to rebuild it. Fifty thousand people returned under the leadership of three men: Zerubbabel, Ezra, and Nehemiah. They rebuilt the city and the temple and restored public worship of God. They lived that way for the next four hundred years. During that time, Persia fell to Greece, then Greece fell to Rome.

Why I Need to Know This

If I don't understand the Old Testament, I may be confused about the story, uncertain where to find things, and unsure that it really makes sense. Unless I see the overall picture, I may dismiss the little pictures in the Old Testament. It gives me confidence that the Bible makes sense, and hope that I can gain a reasonable understanding of it.

Rome was ruling that part of the world when Jesus was born and the New Testament began.

That sums up the Old Testament. I have left out a few details, but in its skeletal form, that is the historical overview. Not so difficult, eh?

The time span is helpful to understand. The first eleven chapters of Genesis record prehistory, and we are not certain how much time passed from Creation to the birth of Abraham. Rounding off the numbers, we find Abraham appearing in Genesis 12 about two thousand years before Christ; Moses, about fifteen hundred years before Christ; David, about a thousand years before Christ; and Ezra about five hundred years before Christ. Some of these figures are "rounder" than others, but they give you the general picture.

The first seventeen books of the Old Testament, called the historical books, tell the basic story. The next five books, books of poetry, and the last seventeen books, books of prophecy, were all written during the same time period as the first seventeen books. That makes thirty-nine books in the Old Testament. If you want to learn the story of the Old Testament, you have to read the first seventeen books. Everything else is, in the broad strokes, supplemental to that information.

Old Testament Time Line					
Pre-history	2000 B.C.	1500 B.C.	1000 B.C.	500 B.C.	
Adam and Eve	Abraham	Moses	David	Ezra	Jesus

Many people find it astonishing that it is so simple. However, details add color and interest, so for the next part of the chapter, I would like to elaborate on that story and fill in some of the gaps. When fleshing out the skeletal framework of the Old Testament, it can be helpful to break the time span of the Old Testament into eras.

FAQ #17

What Are the Major Eras of Old Testament History?

The entire story of the Old Testament can be divided into nine major time periods.

1. Creation Era (Genesis 1-11)

God created the universe, the world, all that is in the world, and humankind. Original creation was a paradise without sin. Adam and Eve lived in perfect fellowship and harmony with God, ruling with God over the Garden of Eden. They were individuals of amazing intellect and stunning beauty, created in the moral, spiritual, and intellectual image of God.

But for reasons that transcend our knowledge and understanding, sin entered the world. Adam and Eve sinned and were driven out of the Garden of Eden. As they and their children multiplied, it became clear that all their descendants inherited their sinful nature. When Adam and Eve fell, all succeeding generations toppled like dominoes.

Humanity became increasingly wicked as the population ballooned. Several hundred years later, by the time of Noah, millions of people dwelt on the earth. God destroyed the earth with a universal flood as a judgment on the sin of humanity, preserving a righteous remnant in Noah and his immediate family.

After the flood, God instructed Noah and his family to spread out and inhabit the whole earth. In direct disobedience to that command, everyone stayed in one place and began building a monument to themselves, called the Tower of Babel. As judgment for this sin and to fulfill the divine mandate to inhabit the whole earth, God caused the people working on the tower to begin speaking different languages. Because they could no longer understand each other, they broke into language groups, and spread out to form the various nations of the world.

2. Patriarch Era (Genesis 12-50)

"Patriarch" means "great father," and the Book of Genesis presents four men who are the patriarchs of Israel. They are Abraham, his son Isaac, Isaac's son Jacob, and Jacob's son Joseph. We will look at each one of them.

God decided to establish a nation that He would bless, and through which He would bless the whole world. He chose Abraham to be the father of this nation, which became Israel. Abraham was living in the city of Ur, near where the Tigris and Euphrates flow into the Persian Gulf, in what is now Iraq. God led him to the land of Canaan, which is now Israel, near the present city of Jerusalem. God made a unilateral covenant with Abraham and promised to give him land, descendants, and divine blessing. Once in Canaan, Abraham had two sons, Ishmael, from a servant girl, and Isaac, from his wife, Sarah.

Isaac was the child of the covenant, meaning that the promises given to Abraham for land, descendants, and divine blessing were passed down to Isaac. Isaac lived in the land of Abraham, enjoying prosperity and a long life. He had two sons, Esau and Jacob. Jacob, as son of the covenant, inherited the promises given to Abraham and Isaac. Jacob was a dishonest and manipulative man during the early years of his life. God finally caught his attention, however, and he developed more purpose to his life. Jacob had twelve sons, and this time, instead of one son being singled out as the son of the covenant, the promises of Abraham, Isaac, and Jacob passed down to all twelve sons who fathered the twelve tribes or clans of Israel. Every Hebrew person can trace his or her ancestry back to one of these twelve sons.

Jacob's next-to-the-youngest of the twelve sons, Joseph, is, nevertheless, the next main figure on whom the book of Genesis focuses. Being Jacob's favorite son caused resentment among his brothers. So they sold him as a slave to a caravan which took him to Egypt. While there, through a series of acts of God, Joseph rose in power to become second-in-command of the entire nation of Egypt, and was used by God to save his family in Canaan from starvation when a severe famine hit. Jacob and all his sons and grandsons moved to Egypt, where they lived for the next four hundred years.

3. Exodus Era (Exodus-Deuteronomy)

Soon after Joseph died, the Egyptians, viewing the Hebrew people as a possible military threat because of how quickly they multiplied, enslaved them. Their lives as slaves were very difficult, and finally God chose Moses to lead them out of Egypt, out of slavery, and back into the land which God had promised to Abraham and his descendants—the modern land of Israel. The Pharaoh, Egypt's ruler, refused the Israelites' request to leave, so God levied on the nation of Egypt a series of ten plagues. These terrible plagues culminated in the death of every first-born child and animal in Egypt except those belonging to the Hebrew people. This finally convinced Pharaoh to let the Hebrew people go.

They had journeyed as far as the Red Sea when Pharaoh changed his mind and chased after them. God parted the Red Sea, the children of Israel made their way across to safety, and the Red Sea flowed together again, killing all of Pharaoh's soldiers. They then marched to the southern tip of the Sinai peninsula and camped at the base of Mt. Sinai, where God gave Moses the Ten Commandments. God's intention was to lead them then into the promised land. But when spies sent to scout Canaan reported giants living in the land, the people rebelled and refused to enter the land, even though God had promised them victory. As a result, they wandered in the wilderness for forty years until that rebellious generation died. Then, God led the new generation into the land.

4. Conquest Era (Joshua)

After Moses led the Israelites out of Egypt, shepherded them for forty years in the wilderness, and brought them to the eastern gateway into the Promised Land (Canaan), he died. His protégé, Joshua, then took over leadership of the nation. He led them into the Promised Land, and through brilliant military leadership, conquered all the fortified cities inside the land which had been promised by God to the Israelites through Abraham. It might seem unfair for the Israelites to displace the people living in that area, but God used Israel as a sword of divine judgment on the Canaanites and other dreadfully degenerate, cruel, evil, and pagan people living there.

5. Judges Era (Judges)

After the conquest of the Promised Land was complete, the people of Israel settled down for the next four hundred years to a relatively normal life as farmers, shepherds, and merchants. Their informal system of government went into effect only if they were threatened militarily by other people. After the land was conquered, the people became spiritually lazy and began violating God's law which had been given to them by Moses. In divine judgment for their sin, God brought a nation to suppress them. This caused the Israelites to cry out to God for deliverance. God gave them a deliverer, who was called a "judge." A political, military and religious person, the judge was blessed by God with extraordinary leadership abilities. This judge would lead the nation in a revival which would move God to bless their military efforts, and they would be released from the bonds of their oppressors. This happened seven times during the four hundred years of the judges. God promised that, if Israel would live in a righteous relationship with Him, He would protect them. If they didn't, God would allow them to become vulnerable to other nations. As their leaders went, so went the nation.

6. Kingdom Era (1 Samuel-2 Chronicles)

Finally, the Israelites appealed to God for a king, and God gave them Saul, their first king, from the tribe of Benjamin. Saul led Israel in righteousness for only a short time. He was removed by God as king (he was actually killed in battle), and David was then made king. David led the nation in righteousness all his life, and the nation prospered as at no other time in its history. David died in peace and prosperity at an old age, and his son, Solomon, became king in his place. Solomon led the nation in righteousness for the first part of his forty-year reign, but then fell into sin.

As a result, when Solomon died, God judged the sin of Israel by allowing the nation to divide into a northern kingdom and a southern kingdom. The northern kingdom kept the name "Israel" since ten of the tribes of Israel remained faithful to it. Ruled by a series of nineteen kings, none of which were righteous, Israel lasted for about two hundred fifty years. As a final act of judgment on the nation for its sin, God allowed Assyria, a powerful neighbor to the northeast, to destroy Israel, and it was never restored again.

The southern kingdom adopted the name Judah, because Judah was the largest of the two tribes which were faithful to the southern kingdom. (Benjamin was the other tribe.) They lasted for about one hundred fifty years after the destruction of the northern kingdom. Of their twenty kings, eight were righteous, which explains why the southern kingdom survived longer than the northern kingdom. Righteousness prolonged the life of the nation. Sin shortened it. However, after four hundred years of existence, the southern kingdom was conquered by a powerful neighbor to the east, Babylonia.

7. The Exile Era (Ezekiel-Daniel)

Babylonia had conquered Assyria to the north and was the most powerful country in the area at that time. Babylonia took many of the Hebrew people into captivity for seventy years.

8. The Return Era (Ezra-Esther)

At the end of this seventy-year period, which was prophesied by the prophet Jeremiah, God brought Persia from the east to conquer Babylonia. The king of Persia saw all the Jewish people living in Babylonia and gave them permission to return to Canaan, rebuild the city of Jerusalem and the temple, and reinstitute temple worship of God. Fifty thousand people returned from Babylonia to Jerusalem under the leadership of three men: Zerubbabel, Ezra, and Nehemiah. Although Israel was never independent again, it did have reasonable autonomy as far as temple worship was concerned.

9. Silence Era (No books of the Bible written during this time)

Four hundred years passed, during which Persia declined as the dominant military power of the day, and Greece emerged. Then Greece declined as the dominant military power of the day, and Rome emerged. Rome was ruling that part of the world when Jesus was born and the New Testament era began.

FAQ #18

Q **What Was the Geographical Movement of the Old Testament?**

A **The geographical focus of the Israelites moved from Ur (where Abraham first lived), to Canaan (patriarchs), to Egypt (slavery), back to Canaan (which became Israel under the monarchy), to Babylonia (captivity), and back to Jerusalem (return).**

We now look at these movements and key locations for each of the nine eras.

1. Creation Era

Creation took place everywhere, of course, but the Fall took place in the Garden of Eden. We can't locate the Garden exactly, but we do know it was near where four rivers merged, two of which still exist today, the Tigris and the Euphrates. This probably puts the Garden of Eden somewhere in the ancient region of Babylonia and in the modern country of Iraq. Nothing in Iraq today resembles even a shadow of the Garden of Eden, but that is a result of the Fall. When sin entered the world, it damaged not only mankind, but the earth as well. What was once a paradise is now a desert.

2. Patriarch Era

God first revealed himself to Abraham when he was living in the city of Ur, just north of the modern Persian Gulf. Abraham migrated west to the area of modern Jerusalem. He lived in that general area for the rest of his life, as did his son Isaac, and Isaac's son, Jacob. Jacob's son, Joseph, was sold into slavery in Egypt and all Jacob's family eventually joined him there.

3. Exodus Era

Moses led the Israelites out of Egypt, across the Red Sea, south to the bottom of the Sinai peninsula, then north to the oasis of Kadesh Barnea. There the nation rebelled, and wandered in the wilderness of Sinai and south and east of the Dead Sea for forty years. Then Moses led them near to where the Jordan River flows into the Dead Sea, and that is where he died.

4. Conquest Era (Joshua)

Joshua led the Israelites into the Promised Land at Jericho and marched westward to the western city of Ai. This cut the land of Canaan in half. They conquered the southern part of Canaan first, before sweeping into the northern part of Canaan.

5. The Judges Era

There is no geographical movement during the Judges Era. The Israelites were consumed with trying to establish themselves in the Promised Land, even while being plagued by occasional military encroachment from their neighbors.

6. The Kingdom Era

When Assyria conquered the northern kingdom of Israel, the land area generally west of the Sea of Galilee and Jordan River was lost, and the people were scattered. When Babylonia conquered the southern kingdom, the land area generally west of the Dead Sea was lost and the leaders were taken into captivity in Babylonia.

7. Exile Era

The exile took the Israelites into Babylon, which was located northeast of Jerusalem, on the Euphrates River, in modern-day Iraq.

There is no geographical movement during the Exile Era since the captive Israelites remained in Babylonia for seventy years. However, near the end of that time, Babylonia was conquered and ruled by Persia.

8. The Return Era

By decree of their new Persian ruler, the return brought fifty thousand Jews back from captivity in Babylonia to Jerusalem, to rebuild the city, the walls, and the temple.

THINKING BACK

The entire story of the Old Testament took place in a geographical setting no larger than the state of Texas. The Promised Land, corresponding roughly to the modern nation of Israel, is only about one hundred thirty miles long and fifty miles wide. When broken down into its parts, with the story stripped of all but the essentials, the history and geography of the Old Testament are fairly simple and easily grasped.

SPEED BUMP!

1. What is the capsule summary of the Old Testament?
The Old Testament is primarily the story of God's dealings with humanity through the nation of Israel.

2. What are the major eras of Old Testament history?
The entire story of the Old Testament can be divided into nine major time periods.

3. What was the geographical movement of the Old Testament?
The geographical focus of the Israelites moved from Ur (where Abraham first lived), to Canaan (patriarchs), to Egypt (slavery), back to Canaan (which became Israel under the monarchy), to Babylonia (captivity), and back to Jerusalem (return).

FAQ #19

What Is the Capsule Summary of the New Testament?

The New Testament is primarily the story of Jesus' dealings with humanity through the church.

The skeletal story line of the New Testament is fairly simple. Jesus was born in Bethlehem near Jerusalem, according to Old Testament prophecy. Then Jesus and His parents, Mary and Joseph, moved back to their hometown in Nazareth in the northern part of the country, just west of the Sea of Galilee. There, with few details from Scripture, Jesus lived an apparently normal childhood and adulthood until He turned thirty. At the age of thirty, the age at which all teachers by Jewish custom began their ministry, Jesus left Nazareth and went to Jerusalem. He began His initial ministry there and the surrounding area of Judea.

Shortly after, He went north to the area around the Sea of Galilee, making Capernaum His home base. Capernaum was located on the north shore of the Sea of Galilee. He conducted much of His three-year ministry while based at Capernaum, although many events did not actually take place in Capernaum, but in the surrounding area. Eventually, He returned to Jerusalem and was crucified. Three days later, He rose from the dead and showed Himself to His disciples several times over the next forty days. Then, with His disciples gathered around Him on the Mount of Olives, just east of Jerusalem, He visibly ascended into heaven.

He had commissioned

> The New Testament is the very best book that ever was or ever will be known in the world.
>
> *Charles Dickens*

His disciples to take the new message of salvation through Christ to Jerusalem, Judea, and Samaria (the surrounding regions), and to the uttermost parts of the earth. The fulfillment of this command focuses primarily on the apostle Paul, who made three missionary journeys to surrounding areas in Asia Minor and Greece. Finally, Paul was arrested and taken to Rome, where he was eventually executed. Enough disciples remained in Jerusalem, Asia Minor, Greece, and Rome, however, that the message not only survived, but mushroomed into a major world religion.

FAQ #20

What Are the Major Eras of New Testament History?

The entire story of the New Testament can be divided into three major time periods.

1. The Gospels Era (Matthew-John)

Many Jews lived in Jerusalem and the surrounding area west of the Sea of Galilee, the Jordan River, and the Dead Sea. They descended from those who had been left there when the Babylonians conquered the southern kingdom, and those who returned from captivity seventy years later.

Several different groups of people lived there, with the city of Jerusalem and the temple being the focal point of their lives. First were the Pharisees, conservative religious leaders of Israel who stringently separated themselves from the Gentiles around them. They had many traditions which they had elevated in importance to the level of Scripture itself. Jesus even accused them of violating Scripture in order to keep their own traditions.

A second group, the Sadducees, led the liberal religious camp. They were more conciliatory toward interaction with Gentiles and less scrupulous about keeping traditions. These "big money" people had decided to get along with everyone in order to prosper personally.

Third were zealots, political fanatics who willingly risked their very lives to overthrow the Romans and set up Israel as a sovereign nation again.

Finally, there were the ordinary citizens, neither Pharisees nor Sadducees nor political fanatics, but common folk trying to put bread on the table, clothing on their backs, and a roof over their heads; people who went to their synagogues and to the temple, and worshiped God the best way they knew how.

All these groups had one thing in common—a deep longing for the coming of the Messiah, the Promised One of the Old Testament who would come and free Israel and set everything right. Each group had a different concept of who the Messiah would be and how He would go about bringing them deliverance. But all of them lived with a heightened messianic expectation.

Whatever their concept of the Messiah, Jesus did not fit it. No one expected a stable-born man from an obscure village, unknown and unrecognized until His thirtieth birthday. In His lifetime, opinion about Him was as widely divided as it is now. Yet the birth of Jesus towers as the great continental divide of history. He is the Mount Everest of history. Everything before Him flows B.C., before Christ; everything after Him flows A.D., *anno Domini*, the year of our Lord. The calendar was changed because of Him; governments changed because of Him; the course of history changed because of Him. And all this, because multiple millions of people have been transformed because of Him.

The first four books of the New Testament—Matthew, Mark, Luke, and John—tell His story. However, while biographical, they are not intended to be complete pictures of His life. They all spend a great deal of time on His birth and death, and almost no time on His first thirty years. Matthew, Mark, and Luke cover much of the same material, underscoring the humanity of Jesus; John's perspective emphasizes His deity. All four Gospels, when superimposed on each other, present only about fifty days of Jesus' active ministry.

The story, however, goes like this: Jesus' birth to the Virgin Mary resulted from a miraculous conception brought about by the Holy Spirit. Both birth and place of birth—Bethlehem of Judea, a small village near Jerusalem—fulfilled an Old Testament prophecy. Although His parents, Mary and Joseph, lived in Nazareth, they had to travel to Bethlehem when a Roman census required Joseph to be registered in the city of his ancestry. The ruler over that part of the country, Herod, wanted to kill Jesus because Herod saw Him as a threat to his throne. So after Jesus was born, Mary and Joseph, being warned in a dream by God, fled to Egypt until Herod died. They then returned to Nazareth, and there Jesus learned the trade of a carpenter and lived an apparently uneventful life until he turned thirty, at which age Jewish men could begin a ministry.

Isaiah prophesied in the Old Testament (Isaiah 40:3-5) that a prophet would precede the coming of the Messiah. That prophet was John the Baptist, who happened to be Jesus' cousin. He urged people to "repent, for the kingdom of heaven is at hand" (Matthew 3:2), and preached that one would come after him whose sandals John would not be worthy to carry (Matthew 3:11). John was baptizing people in the Jordan River near the Dead Sea, and Jesus went there to have John baptize Him. Upon His being baptized, the heavens opened and He saw the Spirit of God descending like a dove and alighting upon Him. Then God the Father spoke from heaven, saying, "This is my beloved Son, in whom I am well pleased" (Matthew 3:16-17).

Afterward, the Holy Spirit led Jesus out into the wilderness, where Satan tempted Him to depart from God's will for His life. Jesus passed that grueling, difficult trial, remaining sinless and validating His

Why I Need to Know This

If I don't know this, I may be confused about the story and uncertain about where to find things in the New Testament. Unless I see the overall picture, I may not see the little pictures in the New Testament. The stories of the Old and New Testaments together give me confidence that the Bible makes sense, and hope that I can gain a reasonable understanding of it.

readiness to make Himself known as the Messiah.

His early ministry began in and around Jerusalem, where the public initially accepted Him. His two-fold message declared first, that He was the predicted Messiah and that people should believe in Him for salvation; and second, that people should pursue genuine righteousness, not the external hypocrisy so common among the religious leaders. In addition, He performed astonishing miracles which lent credibility to His message and had the people of the entire area talking about Him.

His initial popularity did not last, however, for two reasons. First, when the religious leaders finally understood that Jesus was condemning their practice of empty religion, they felt threatened by the message and jealous of His growing popularity. Therefore, they tried to find ways of opposing Him. Second, it became apparent that many of the people who followed Him were doing so not because they truly believed the message He was proclaiming, but because His miracles intrigued or benefited them.

Because of a growing resistance to His message, Jesus began spending more and more time with just His twelve disciples, preparing them to carry on without Him. At the same time, He challenged the multitudes to count the cost of following Him. Although Jesus traveled quite a bit during this time, His home base was Capernaum.

The Jewish people became more and more polarized about Jesus. The warnings to the multitudes to count the cost of following Him caused the people either to follow Him enthusiastically or resent Him deeply. Finally, during the time of a Jewish holiday when many Jews were in Jerusalem, the religious leaders, jealous of His following and threatened by Jesus' growing attacks on their hypocrisy, stirred up the multitudes to demand Jesus' crucifixion. They subjected Him to a series of unjust trials based on false charges. Pilate, the Roman ruler of Jerusalem, did not want to convict Him, but public sentiment ran so deep that to do otherwise might risk a riot. Since that would not look good on Pilate's record as governor, he conceded and ordered Jesus' crucifixion.

Jesus was executed and buried, lay in the tomb for three days, and then rose from the dead. He presented Himself to His disciples to prove to them that He was alive, told them that He would soon be leaving, and commissioned them to spread the gospel of salvation by grace through faith in Jesus to the entire world.

2. The Church Era (Acts 1-8)

Having completed the preparations for His departure, Jesus ascended into heaven from the Mount of Olives with His followers gathered around Him. He had instructed His disciples to wait in Jerusalem until they were given power from on high, after which they were to witness about Him to the world world.

Ten days after Jesus' ascension into heaven, the church was born in Jerusalem. The disciples were assembled together in a house on the Jewish feast day of Pentecost when the Holy Spirit suddenly came upon them. A sound like a violent, rushing wind filled the place, and flames like fire rested on each one of them, and they began speaking in different tongues as they were filled with the Holy Spirit. These tongues were foreign languages, and when this noise occurred, a large crowd from many different countries gathered at the house, and heard the followers of Jesus each speaking in the listener's own language. Many other miracles happened in the early days of the church, and converts to Christianity increased rapidly.

The multitude of believers had to be organized. Many of the Jews who joined the young church came from other countries. They had left their homes and livelihood to go to Jerusalem for the holiday of Pentecost, and perhaps had run out of money. Some of those who had possessions sold them and brought the money to the apostles to care for those in need. Special people called "deacons" were to look after the physical needs of the early converts while the apostles looked after their spiritual needs.

The animosity that the religious leaders had toward Jesus was now directed toward the increasing number of his followers. They arrested Stephen, who was one of the deacons, for preaching about Jesus. They tried to get him to deny Jesus, but he would not, so they stoned him to death. Thus Stephen became the first known martyr of the church.

3. The Missions Era (Acts 9-28)

One of the most vicious persecutors of the early Christians was a Pharisee named Saul. After creating havoc among the Christians in Jerusalem, he left for Damascus in Syria to find and persecute Christians there. On the way, Jesus appeared to him in a blinding vision, and Saul was converted to Christianity. His name was changed to Paul, and he became the greatest missionary of that time, ministering to the Gentiles. In three missionary journeys to Asia Minor and Greece, Paul was used by God to lead many Gentiles to Christ and to establish many churches throughout the region.

The first missionary journey, a two-year trip, took him to Galatia in Asia Minor (modern Turkey). On the second missionary journey, one that lasted three years, he travelled to Macedonia in modern Greece. And finally, his third missionary trip traversed Asia, a region in modern Turkey where he ministered for four years. On all three missionary journeys he left from Antioch, a town in Asia Minor very near the Syrian border.

Paul then returned to Jerusalem, where he was arrested on false charges. A Roman citizen, he appealed to Rome to plead his case before Caesar. The Bible does not give us the final details, but we think that Paul died in Rome, having been executed for the false charges.

Most of the remaining books of the New Testament were written by Paul, Peter, or John during the time period covered in the Book of Acts. However, while providing much needed instructions for the Christian life, they generally don't provide much more about the story of the church.

FAQ #21

Q **What Was the Geographical Movement of the New Testament?**

A **The geographical focus of the New Testament moved from Bethlehem to Jerusalem, to Capernaum, back to Jerusalem, then to Asia Minor and Greece.**

Let us now look at these movements and key locations for each era.

1. The Gospels Era

The geographical movement in the Gospels Era followed Jesus' life. Shortly after He was born in Bethlehem, He fled with His parents to Egypt. When it was safe to come back into Palestine after the death of Herod, who tried to kill Him, they went home to Nazareth. Jesus lived there until He began His ministry around Jerusalem. Then, He moved north to Capernaum, and made His home there for much of His ministry. Then, as the final events of His life began to draw to a climax, His travels took Him to Jerusalem. He died and arose there, and ascended to heaven from that area.

2. The Church Era

There is no geographical movement during the Church Era, since the church remained close to Jerusalem until persecution began, which ushered in the Missions Era.

3. The Missions Era

The geographical movement in the Missions Era followed the missionary journeys of Paul. His first missionary journey took him to Galatia in modern Turkey. He returned to Jerusalem for a time before embarking on his second missionary journey. This took him back to Galatia and on to Macedonia in modern Greece, after which he returned to Jerusalem.

His final missionary journey took him to Asia near the Aegean Sea in modern Turkey, and back to Jerusalem. Then, he went to Rome to defend himself against false charges, where he died.

THINKING BACK

The entire story of the Gospels took place in a geographical setting not much larger than the state of Connecticut. Jesus' travels, for the most part, did not exceed the distance from Jerusalem to Capernaum, about eighty miles north to south, and from the Sea of Galilee to Nazareth, about ten or fifteen miles east to west.

The apostle Paul traveled nearly fifteen hundred miles on his third missionary journey, and nearly two thousand miles on his trip to Rome.

The story of the New Testament, like the Old, when stripped to its essentials, is fairly simple.

SPEED BUMP!

1. What is the capsule summary of the New Testament?
The New Testament is primarily the story of Jesus' dealings with humanity through the church.

2. What are the major eras of New Testament history?
The entire story of the New Testament can be divided into three major time periods.

3. What was the geographical movement of the New Testament?
The geographical focus of the New Testament moved from Bethlehem to Jerusalem, to Capernaum, back to Jerusalem, then to Asia Minor and Greece.

FAQ #22

 What Is the Message of the Bible?

 The message of the Bible is that God is demonstrating, to the universe through us, that He is who He says He is.

God says that He is all-knowing, all-powerful, everywhere present simultaneously;

> I want to know one thing—the way to heaven; how to land safe on that happy shore. God Himself has condescended to teach the way: For this very end He came from heaven. He hath written it down in a book. O give me that book! At any price, give me the book of God! I have it: Here is knowledge enough for me. Let me be a man of one book.
>
> *John Wesley*

that He is loving, merciful, and just. Many people would say that the evidence around us proves just the opposite—that either He does not care about the suffering of humanity or that He cannot do anything about it. Someone once said that the fact that celery is good for you, but hot fudge is bad for you, proves there is no God. We are supposed to smile at such a comment, but there is a deep and subtle truth behind it.

God wants to prove that, in spite of apparent evidence to the contrary, He is perfect in His character and able to perform whatever He chooses. In spite of the pain, suffering, and injustice we see in the world, God is who He says He is.

In demonstrating to the universe through us that God is who He says He is, His goal is to bring glory to Himself and pleasure to us. The Westminster Confession, a seventeenth-century statement of faith still used in many churches today, states that the chief end of man is to glorify God and enjoy Him forever. This startling statement negates the concept of God as a cosmic killjoy, and brings up several questions. First, who does God say He is? Second, how does He demonstrate through us that He is who He says He is? Third, why does God want to be glorified; and fourth, how does man enjoy Him forever?

Who Does God Say He Is?

Another volume in this series, *Just the FAQs About God*, treats this topic more fully. Nevertheless, we can summarize the answer here. God says He is the eternal supreme being, the creator of the universe. He is holy, loving, just, merciful, unchanging, all-knowing, all-powerful, and present everywhere simultaneously.

Holy defines God as without sin, without corruption, without contamination of anything that is not good. For God to be loving means that He desires nothing but good for us. For Him to be just means, in part, that He applies penalties for sin equally to everyone without partiality. It also means that if a penalty is paid, punishment is rescinded. God as merciful means that He offers a way of escape to those who deserve judgment. As He expresses these moral characteristics, He does so without ever changing and with full knowledge, power, and presence to do whatever He wills.

How Does He Demonstrate through Us that He Is Who He Says He Is?

God created the universe to be a paradise in which He would live in fellowship with humanity. However, sin contaminated humanity and all the rest of creation. The Bible does not tell us how or why this defilement first occurred. The sin of Adam and Eve goes back to the temptation of Satan, but two questions persist: Why did Adam and Eve sin if they were living in fellowship with God in paradise? And where did sin come from in the first place? We don't know the answer to those questions. We know sin originated with Satan, a once-righteous angel who served God. But the Bible simply says that one day, sin was found in him (Ezekiel 28:15). It doesn't say where the sin came from, or why God ever allowed it, or why God didn't destroy Satan before he had a chance to contaminate humanity. Scholars have debated these questions for centuries. While we can offer educated and wise speculation, we cannot say for sure because the Bible does not tell us.

God has revealed Himself to us simply to make friends with us.

How does He demonstrate, through us, that He is who He says He is? To answer that question, we must simply start from where we are. Sin exists. It entered the world through Adam and Eve when they were living in the Garden of Eden. As a result, everyone who would ever be born would be contaminated by sin. That contamination ends in spiritual death—eternal separation from God. Why? Because a holy God cannot abide the presence of sin, and because He is just, He applies the penalty of sin equally to all. However, because God is also merciful and loving, He did not want to leave humanity in its sin. Therefore, He sent His own Son to die for us. Since Jesus became a man, He could die. Because He was God, He never sinned, and His righteousness could extend to others. His one life could save all lives from eternal separation from God. His righteousness, knowledge, power, and presence were enough to satisfy the penalty for sin, for everyone, for all time.

Therefore, God's plan is to redeem us from sin and restore humanity to a righteous relationship with Him through Jesus. It is a demonstration through us to the universe that not only benefits humanity, but it also manifests that He is who He says He is (Colossians 2:13-15).

To glorify God means simply to tell the truth about Him.

Why Does God Want to Be Glorified?

We don't know all the reasons why God wants to bring glory to Himself. God certainly deserves glory because of the perfection of His being. But does that qualify Him as a cosmic egomaniac? That is what some cynics claim. How do we avoid that perception?

For God to glorify Himself simply means to call accurate attention to who He is. When we glorify God, we simply tell the truth about God. When we live in a way that glorifies God, we are living demonstrations and mouthpieces of the truth about God. God is the greatest of all beings, perfect in character, and capable of doing whatever He wishes. He wishes to do good for us. It is that simple. That is one reason He desires to bring glory to Himself.

What is the alternative for God or for us? Should God lie about Himself? Should we lie about God? God's desire to be glorified is not the result of an inflated ego. Rather, it is His desire for us to know the truth about Him, so that we can avoid the Great Negative—misery in this life and then die and going to hell. He wants us to experience the Great Positive—joy in this life and then die and go to heaven.

Humanity benefits when God is glorified, because then we know the truth. Where that truth is acknowledged, proclaimed, and cherished, life becomes increasingly like the life God intended us to experience when He created us. It becomes increasingly like the life He wants us to experience forever in heaven. It allows us to become increasingly like God.

The reverse happens also: For humanity not to glorify God is to accept the most fundamental deception, to suppress the most fundamental truth, and to drift into the fog of confusion and evil, for evil thrives in falsehood, error, and untruth.

Not to glorify God is to poison life so that it becomes increasingly like hell. Everything about God is good, and everything that is not true of God is bad. The closer a person is to being like God, the better off he is. The less like God a person is, the worse off he is. So we don't have to visualize God as some cosmic egomaniac, demanding adulation at the expense of others. Rather, His glory results in just the opposite.

We see a great example of this in Isaiah 6:1-8. God reveals himself in great glory:

In the year that King Uzziah died, I saw the LORD sitting on a throne, high and lifted up, and the train of His robe filled the temple. Above it stood seraphim; each one had six wings; with two he covered his face, with two he covered his feet, and with two he flew. And one cried to another and said:

"Holy, holy, holy is the LORD of hosts;
The whole earth is full of His glory!"

And the posts of the door were shaken by the voice of him who cried out, and the house was filled with smoke. (vv. 1-4).

Based on the glory of God which Isaiah witnessed, he knew that God was holy and he was unholy. His unholiness cut him off from God. He was terrified, and he repented deeply:

Not to glorify God is to promote deception and to poison life so it becomes like hell.

So I said:
"Woe is me, for I am undone!
Because I am a man of unclean lips,
And I dwell in the midst of a people of unclean lips;
For my eyes have seen the King,
The Lord of hosts." (v. 5).

Because Isaiah repented, his sins were forgiven, and he was cleansed and restored to fellowship with God

Then one of the seraphim flew to me, having in his hand a live coal which he had taken with tongs from the altar. And he touched my mouth with it, and said:

"Behold, this has touched your lips; your iniquity is taken away, and your sin purged" (vv. 6-7).

Because Isaiah repented and was restored to fellowship with God, he could now be used by God on a scale that was not possible before:

Also I heard the voice of the Lord, saying:
"Whom shall I send,
And who will go for Us?"
Then I said, "Here am I! Send me" (v. 8).

God revealed His glory to Isaiah. That glory caused Isaiah to see the truth: God was holy and he was unholy. He repented of his unholiness, was forgiven, restored to fellowship with God, and used greatly by Him. Perceiving God's glory gives us an opportunity to repent, which demonstrates the goodness of God, for He is "not willing that any should perish but that all should come to repentance" (2 Peter 3:9).

I don't mean that we come to God simply for reasons of personal comfort. It is much deeper than that. But as far as God's motivation is concerned, this understanding destroys the misconception that He is a heartless cosmic ego-

God's glory illuminates truth that moves us to repentance and the pleasure of fellowship with Him.

maniac, requiring obeisance from humanity even though that obeisance is hurtful to them. That is like some volcano god who requires the sacrifice of a virgin to him every spring or else he will spew molten lava all over the village. We want to avoid that misconception. God is not so small.

On the other hand, the desire to avoid pain and to pursue pleasure is not to be ignored. God tells us about hell, its misery and torment, and implores us to accept Him so that we don't have to go there. He also tells us about the glories and pleasures of heaven, so that we will want to go there. To want pain and to avoid pleasure is unnatural. God has created us for pleasure and not for pain. Pain signals that something is wrong. That is why He has done everything in His power, short of destroying our wills, to get us to receive Him. He wants us to live with Him forever in heaven.

Much pain we experience comes simply from our existence in a fallen world.

A second misconception I want to avoid is the notion that all pain we experience in this life comes about because we have failed God somehow. If that were the case, Jesus' pain on the cross would be a result of His failure. That is impossible, because Jesus was without sin or shortcoming of any kind. No, Christians suffer in this world because it is a fallen world, and until all sin and evil are destroyed, we will become casualties to it. Christians will still get diseases, just as non-Christians do. We will still have accidents, and be maltreated, just as non-Christians are. Many of us experience unavoidable pain simply because we live in a fallen world.

Beyond the unavoidable pain, however, we can prevent much pain that is avoidable by living in close fellowship and trusting obedience to God. Sin triggers a powerful law of cause and effect. The apostle Paul wrote in Galatians 6:7-8, "Do not be deceived, God is not mocked; for whatever a man sows, that he will also reap. For he who sows to his flesh will of the flesh reap corruption, but he who sows to the Spirit will of the Spirit reap everlasting life."

If you sow anger, you reap anger. If you sow sexual immorality, you reap physical and psychological damage; if you sow selfishness, you reap loneliness, and so on. The closer one lives to God, the more he will reap the fruit of the Spirit: love, joy, peace, patience, kindness, goodness, faithfulness, gentleness, self-control (Galatians 5:22-23). In the next world, of course, nothing but pleasure exists for the child of God, and nothing but pain persists for the one who rejects God. All humankind will either reap pleasure in heaven or harvest pain in hell.

So God is not being selfish when He wants to bring glory to Himself. We may not be able to understand all the reasons why God desires to bring glory to Himself, but the ultimate good of humanity is surely one we can all happily accept.

How Do Humans Enjoy God Forever?

We have already answered it, but let's set it in another context to emphasize it. We enjoy God by being like God. Let me give you a true example (the names and circumstances have been changed). Some friends of mine, Bill and Susan, are rural, quiet, uncomplicated, hard-working Christians of uncommon integrity, spiritual depth, and insight. Some years ago, they adopted a twelve-year-old Korean-American boy from San Francisco named Lee. His mother was a prostitute and his father unknown. He lived primarily in the streets, was often abused, never had enough to eat, was perpetually dirty, loud, aggressive, and careless. When Lee came to live with Bill and Susan, his circumstances changed radically. From city to country, from no family to a close family, from poverty to plenty, from dirty to clean, from unstructured to structured, from no responsibility to much responsibility, from sloppy to tidy, from no discipline to discipline, from unchristian to Christian—if he had been brought from the back side of the moon, the difference would not have been greater.

Why I Need to Know This

I need to know this because understanding the Bible is more than just becoming acquainted with the people, places, and events. A greater message transcends the story, and that greater message is what must ultimately find a home in my heart.

Although Lee was glad to be out of San Francisco, his new life in the country disconcerted him. He disliked the structure, discipline, and work, but he appreciated the safety and positively reveled in three meals a day, a warm bed, and clean clothes. Lee immediately modified his behavior. He became reserved, polite, cautious, and friendly. It was his way of playing it safe.

But then, as he relaxed in a safe, loving environment, a transformation took place. As he developed over the next few years into a powerfully built young man, he lost the politeness, caution, and friendliness induced by insecurity. As he shed his insecurity, his real personality reasserted itself. He became quiet, sullen, withdrawn, moody, belligerent, and uncooperative. This personality shift caused confusion and heartache for Bill and Susan. Everything had been going well, and they thought Lee had adapted happily to his new life.

> The more God transforms us into His likeness, the more we enjoy Him.

However, they continued to love and accept him while at the same time requiring respectful and responsible speech and behavior. If he complied, things went smoothly; if he didn't, there was always a price to pay, commensurate with the infraction. They were remarkably consistent. "Lee," they would tell him, "we love you as our own son, we will do whatever is in our power to make your life better. We will never stop loving you. But you must understand that we will not accept belligerent behavior, irresponsibility, or immorality. If you break the rules, you must pay the consequences." They exhibited an almost superhuman example of the balance of love and discipline which Dr. James Dobson presents in his book *Dare to Discipline*.

For some time, their discipline did not seem to be working. Lee became particularly rebellious, so Bill and Susan sent him to a summer camp for troubled teenagers. "Lee, we are doing this because we love you, and think that this camp will help you. When you come back, if you willingly fit in and uphold your responsibilities in the family, we will meet you halfway. But if you insist on rebelling against your life here, we will have to send you back," they told him.

Bill and Susan had deep convictions from the Bible about what

God required of them as parents. Through all the heartache, they stuck to their guns. The change was not dramatic, but slowly, as Lee grew to maturity, the impact of Bill and Susan's unconditional love and consistent discipline brought its reward. Lee began to see the futility of his way of life, and the deep richness of Bill and Susan's. He changed from the inside out, and committed his life to Christ.

A man now, Lee is happy, polite, quiet, gentle, disciplined, responsible, courteous, and friendly. The transformation is remarkable. And make no mistake about it—Lee understands his incredibly good fortune in being adopted by Bill and Susan and the remarkable transformation they brought about in him. He practically worships the ground they walk on. When they are together, security, purpose, meaning, belonging, happiness, joy, warmth, and laughter mark their relationship. Bill and Susan delight in Lee. Lee enjoys Bill and Susan, and the more Lee becomes like Bill and Susan, the more he enjoys them.

To enjoy God forever is a concept beyond our full comprehension. It does not mean enjoying God as you would a roller-coaster ride, or a new car, or a job promotion. But it surely includes enjoying God by becoming less like what He isn't, and more like what He is. When we experience or imagine the best friendships or "loves" on earth, I think we glimpse how we will enjoy God in heaven forever. Unity, meaning, purpose, love, acceptance, and belonging characterize the relationship. It never wears thin, it never grows stale. When God fills the deepest longings of our soul, we can enjoy Him, and all the implications of that, forever.

FAQ #23

 What Is the Focus of the Old Testament?

 The Old Testament focuses on the temporary solution God provided to humanity's sin problem.

Sin, and only sin, separates and alienates humanity from God and prevents our enjoying Him. Therefore, the sin problem needs to be dealt with to reconcile humanity to God. Humanity must find a way for its sin to be forgiven. God Himself provided His sinless Son to die in our place, so that Jesus' death could count for ours, Jesus' life could be given to us, and Jesus' righteousness attributed to us. Of course, Jesus the Son was not given to us until New Testament times. During the time of the Old Testament, God established a system of sacrifice and worship that pictured or foreshadowed the reality to come. In this way, He demonstrated to the world through Israel that He was who He said He was.

Unconfessed sin keeps us from enjoying God.

Separation from God through sin is called "death" (Romans 6:23). God pictured this spiritual reality in the Old Testament through a system of animal sacrifice. It is important to understand what the sacrificial system did and what it did not do. The prophet Samuel said, "To obey is better than sacrifice, and to heed than the fat of rams" (1 Samuel 15:22 NASB). David said, in Psalm 51:16-17, "You do not desire sacrifice, or else I would give it; You do not delight in burnt offering. The sacrifices of God are a broken spirit, a broken and a contrite heart—These, O God, You will not despise."

Merely sacrificing animals to God does not take away sins. God requires repentance in order to forgive sins. Jesus called the Pharisees in the New Testament "white-washed sepulchers" because they kept up the proper appearance on the outside, but inside they were unrepentant. But if you were repentant, God prescribed sacrifices which you were to offer. These, always costly, usually included the death of an animal, which portrayed actual death. They reminded people graphically of the true cost and consequences of sin. The physical picture simulated the spiritual and ultimate result of sin—eternal death.

This visual aid helps us understand what was at stake with our sin and what it would take in order for us to have our sins forgiven permanently. If we did not want to have to offer animal sacrifices throughout eternity, something had to happen permanently to remove the need. That "something" was the sacrificial death of Jesus, upon which the New Testament focuses.

FAQ #24

What is the Focus of the New Testament?

The New Testament focuses on the permanent solution God has provided in Christ to humanity's sin problem.

What the Old Testament pictured, the New Testament presents in reality. In the Old Testament, sacrificed lambs covered the sins of Israel temporarily until they could be taken away permanently. In the New Testament, the Lamb of God, Jesus, was sacrificed so that all sins could be forgiven permanently. Jesus' death, entirely adequate to take away the sins of the whole world, actually affects only those who accept His offer of forgiveness, repent of their sins, and follow Him. Jesus meant, when He said that He had "fulfilled" the law, that no longer was it necessary to keep sacrificing bulls and goats and sheep. Now humanity needed only to rely on the Great Sacrifice of Calvary.

The message in the New Testament has nothing to do with sacrificing animals but with believing in Jesus. Jesus Himself commissioned His disciples to "Go, therefore, and make disciples of all the nations, baptizing them in the name of the Father and of the Son and of the Holy Spirit, teaching them to observe all things that I have commanded you; and lo, I am with you always, even to the end of the age" (Matthew 28:19-20). Jesus wants Christians to commit themselves to spreading the message of salvation by grace through faith in Him to everyone in the world.

THINKING BACK

Let me draw the loose ends together in summary. The message of the Bible is that God continuously demonstrates, to the universe through us, that He is who He says He is. He is perfect in moral character and unlimited in His ability to do what He chooses. The perfection of His moral character does not allow Him to ignore sin, yet it propels Him to offer the ultimate sacrifice Himself in order to provide a way for us to escape the penalty of our sin. His immeasurable power executes His plan that provides for our escape. In addition, as Packer said, God wants to make friends with us. He wants to be in a close relationship with us, finding His joy in giving us gifts and we finding our joy in giving Him our worship and thanks. That is God's end for us. Friendship between two persons has no further motive. It is an end in itself. It almost sounds too good to be true! In fact, some have suggested that, not only is the chief end of man to glorify God *and* enjoy Him forever, but rather, our chief end is to glorify God *by* enjoying Him forever. *That* is good news! That is the Bible's message.

SPEED BUMP!

1. **What is the message of the Bible?**
The message of the Bible is that God is demonstrating, to the universe through us, that He is who He says He is.

2. **What is the focus of the Old Testament?**
The Old Testament focuses on the temporary solution God provided to humanity's sin problem.
3. **What is the focus of the New Testament?**
The New Testament focuses on the permanent solution God has provided in Christ to humanity's sin problem.

FOR FURTHER STUDY

Scripture Passages

- Matthew 28:19-20
- Ephesians 1
- Hebrews 9:12-15
- Hebrews 10:1-18
- Hebrews 10:19-25

FAQ #25

What Is God's Strategy for Relating to Humanity?

Four main elements comprise God's strategy for relating to humanity: revelation, faith, blessing, and reproduction.

1. God Reveals Truth to Humanity

In the earliest days, He revealed truth directly, through one-on-one contact, dreams and visions, or angel messengers. Now, He reveals truth primarily through the Bible.

2. God Asks People To Live by Faith

God's requests take people in the opposite direction of their natural inclinations. They respond only if they believe God. Believing something you can't see is the nature of faith. You act on something contrary to your nature. You subordinate your own instincts to Someone you believe has greater wisdom.

3. God Blesses the Faithful

As individuals live for God by faith, trusting God and obeying Him as best they know how, God blesses them, and gives them a deeply satisfying quality of life.

4. Others Desire To Know God

Finally, when others look at the Christian and see the blessing that comes to him through his relationship with God, they become thirsty to know God also.

These principles worked themselves out in the Old Testament differently than they did in the New Testament. We will look at

> Defend the Bible? I would just as soon defend a lion. Just turn the Bible loose. It will defend itself.
>
> *Charles H. Spurgeon*

each of these principles (revelation, faith, blessing, and reproduction) and see how they functioned in the Old and New Testaments.

FAQ #26

 How Was God's Strategy for Relating to Humanity Executed in the Old Testament?

 God worked through the nation of Israel, promising earthly reward for trusting obedience.

Revelation

God revealed Himself to people in the Old Testament in different ways. In the era before Scripture, God used miraculous means, but after portions of the Old Testament were recorded, the people had the benefit of Scripture.

This revelation required the Old Testament people to act in ways that departed from normal behavior. For example, they were not to amass horses as military resources. God promised to protect them from all enemies and fight for them as long as they remained righteous.

They were to refrain from labor or commerce every seventh day. Every seventh year, they were to let their land lie fallow to rest it. God promised to bless their business and agricultural pursuits to such an extent that they would have plenty even throughout that seventh year.

They were to give almost 30 percent of their income in tithes and offerings for national taxes and for the functioning of the sacrificial and priestly systems. God promised to prosper them economically if they would obey these commands.

Faith

If you believed that an invisible God would protect you from enemies, you would be willing to forego the development of a cavalry and chariots for warfare. If you did not trust God to protect you, you would disobey and raise all the horses you could to protect yourself.

If you believed that an invisible God would prosper your farming to such an extent that you could actually not plant one year out of seven, and spend that year in praise to the Lord, you would obey, and forego planting the seventh year. If you did not trust God to prosper you, you would disobey, and raise all the crops you could to supply yourself.

If you believed that God would prosper you financially, so that you could afford to give 30 percent of your money for national and religious purposes, you would obey and tithe your income. If you didn't trust God to prosper you, you would disobey, and keep the money for yourself.

God's revelation took man in the opposite direction from his natural inclinations to protect himself, supply himself, and fund himself. Faith requires that you believe God and do things His way.

Blessing

God blesses living by faith.

If the Israelites would trust God to meet their needs, and obey His commandments, God promised to give them, not just subsistence, but abundance beyond comprehension in every area of their national life.

Why I Need to Know This

I need to know this in order to understand how God works in my life. I might think that some Old Testament blessings should be coming to me as a result of my faithful obedience to God, or fear that God is displeased with me for something that I don't know. I might expect things from God that He hasn't promised a New Testament believer. I also need to know how God links revelation, faith, and blessing to the evangelization of the world. What I believe matters, but so does how I live.

Now it shall be, if you will diligently obey the LORD your God, being careful to do all His commandments which I command you today, the LORD your God will set you high above all the nations of the earth. And all these blessings shall come upon you and overtake you, if you will obey the LORD your God.

Blessed shall you be in the city, and blessed shall you be in the country. Blessed shall be the offspring of your body and the produce of your ground and the offspring of your beasts, the increase of your herd and the young of your flock. Blessed shall be your basket and your kneading bowl. Blessed shall you be when you come in, and blessed shall you be when you go out.

The LORD will cause your enemies who rise up against you to be defeated before you; they shall come out against you one way, and shall flee before you seven ways. The LORD will command the blessing upon you in your barns and in all that you put your hand to, and He will bless you in the land which the LORD your God gives you.

The LORD will establish you as a holy people to Himself, as He swore to you, if you will keep the commandments of the LORD your God, and walk in His ways. So all the peoples of the earth shall see that you are called by the name of the LORD, and they shall be afraid of you (Deuteronomy 28:1-10 NASB).

God always ties blessings to obedience to His commands.

God put His word on the line in precise terms. Marvelous blessings would be theirs if they fully obeyed His commandments.

Reproduction

God did not choose the nation of Israel to the exclusion of all other peoples. He chose Israel in order to reach all nations. God's idea was to so bless Israel that the world would see the thumbprint of God on their national life, and desire to know God because of the quality of life He had given Israel.

Psalm 67 states this succinctly:

God be gracious to us and bless us,
And cause His face to shine upon us–
That Thy way may be known on the earth,
Thy salvation among all nations.
Let the peoples praise Thee, O God;
Let all the peoples praise Thee.
Let the nations be glad and sing for joy.
For Thou wilt judge the peoples with uprightness,
And guide the nations on the earth.
Let the peoples praise Thee, O God;
Let all the peoples praise Thee.
The earth has yielded its produce;
God, our God, blesses us.
God blesses us,
That all the ends of the earth may fear Him (Psalm 67:1-7 NASB).

There it is in black and white. God blesses Israel that all the ends of the earth may fear (respect or revere) Him.

God always tied blessing to obedience to His commandments. Israel, however, never succeeded in living righteously for very long. The longest sustained period of righteousness for the nation over-lapped David's and the first part of Solomon's reigns, a period of perhaps 60 years. It resulted in the period of greatest national blessing. This stupendous era noticeably affected the surrounding nations.

We read in 1 Kings 10 that word of the splendor of Israel and the wisdom of Solomon spread, even to the queen of Sheba. So fascinated was she by the reports of Israel's grandeur that she came for a closer look. Solomon displayed to her his palace, the city of Jerusalem, and the temple, one of the most glorious buildings ever built.

After the queen had seen everything, the Bible says in verse 5 that "there was no more spirit in her." In other words, she swooned! "It was a true report which I heard in my own land about your words and your wisdom," she said. "Nevertheless, I did not believe the reports until I came and my eyes had seen it. And behold, the half was not told me. You exceed in wisdom and prosperity the report which I heard.

Then she broke out in spontaneous eulogy to God. "Blessed be the LORD your God" (1 Kings 10:6-9 NASB).

This was the way it was supposed to work. The people of the world see the splendor of Israel, and their attention is drawn to God.

FAQ #27

How Was God's Strategy for Relating to Humanity Executed in the New Testament?

God worked through the church, promising spiritual reward for trusting obedience.

God's dealings with the nation of Israel were very much physical, and were designed to picture or foreshadow the spiritual truths which would be presented in the New Testament. The Old Testament sacrificial system foreshadowed, in literal terms, the spiritual work which would be done by Christ on the cross in the New Testament. The beauty of the temple portrayed the glory of God. The physical blessing of protection and food depicted the spiritual protection and nourishment which is ours in Christ.

The blessings in the Old Testament were conspicuously material and physical—the fruit of the vine—although these by no means ruled out spiritual blessings for which the Psalms give earnest praise. The blessings in the New Testament are also conspicuously spiritual—the fruit of the spirit—although material blessings are not ruled out.

Revelation

The revelation from God in the New Testament differs from that in the Old Testament. Christ said that He came to fulfill the Law. Now that He has come and died for our sins and has risen again from the dead, the sacrificial system and the observance of the Mosaic Law are no longer needed. For example, we no longer refrain from planting during the seventh year as we did in the physical kingdom because the physical kingdom has been superseded by the spiritual kingdom it represented.

Nevertheless, the nature of the revelation remains the same. It asks us to function in a way contrary to our natural inclinations: To keep our life, we must lose it; to be great, we must become servants; to be strong, we must be gentle. It is better to give than to receive. Pursue the kingdom of God first, and all our material needs will be met. Reality in the New Testament resides in the invisible, while that which is visible may often deceive us. We must live for the next world instead of this one. As C. S. Lewis said, when we shoot for the next world, we get this one too; but if we shoot for this one, we lose them both.

Faith

To successfully and obediently go against our natural inclinations requires faith. If we believe that God will exalt us if we humble ourselves, then we try to refrain from competing with others. If we believe that the anger of man cannot co-exist with the righteousness of God, then we work on giving our anger over to God, as we trust in His sovereignty. If we believe that God will feed and clothe us (not in great abundance, as was promised in the Old Testament), then we will give sacrificially to spread the gospel. If we believe God, we obey His commands. The opposite of obedience is not disobedience but unbelief. When we lack faith, we disobey.

> **The opposite of obedience is not disobedience but unbelief.**

Blessing

In the Old Testament, God blessed the Israelites with material abundance—the fruit of the vine. In the New Testament, God blesses the church with spiritual abundance—the fruit of the Spirit: love, joy, peace, patience, kindness, goodness, faithfulness, gentleness, self-control (Galatians 5:22-23). When asked what they want out of life, most people will say, "I just want to be happy." To the happy person, life has meaning. The blessing promised to the faithful child of God in the New Testament far exceeds that: peace, love, joy.

Reproduction

In the Old Testament, God promised to raise Israel above the other nations of the world by bestowing material abundance. In the New Testament, He promised to elevate individual Christians above the world by pouring out spiritual blessing. "Let your light so shine before men in such a way that they may see your good works, and glorify your Father who is in heaven" (Matthew 5:16 NASB). "Do all things without grumbling or disputing; that you may prove yourselves to be blameless and innocent, children of God above reproach in the midst of a crooked and perverse generation, among whom you appear as lights in the world" (Philippians 2:14-15 NASB). Our inner spiritual overflow, rather than our outer material wealth, manifests God to the world.

When we live as we should, our lives call attention to the Lord and encourage others to become Christians. "A new commandment I give to you, that you love one another, even as I have loved you, that you also love one another. By this all men will know that you are My disciples, if you have love for one another" (John 13:34-35 NASB). As Christ is accurately portrayed and proclaimed to the world, people will be drawn to Him to become Christians.

FAQ #28

Q **What Are the Consequences of Faithful Obedience to God?**

A **Our faithful obedience to God results in God's glory, our blessing, and a witness to the world.**

Our proper relationship to God centers on faith. Having faith is the only thing we can do, and still do nothing. It is the one response we can make and still not be responsible for saving ourselves.

By faith, we become God's spiritual children. And by faith, we read His revelation, believe it, and respond accordingly. In doing so, we become eligible for His spiritual blessing, which has three primary consequences:

1. *God is glorified.* **As we strive to live in trust and obedience to God according to the Scriptures, our lives gradually take on the character of God Himself. When this happens, the world gets an accurate picture of who God really is because it sees Him in us. The value and worth of God becomes publicly known, and in this way God is glorified.**

2. *Believers are satisfied.* **We who are His spiritual children experience the pleasure of the life which God grants us. Peace, love, and joy become ours in increasing measure even in the midst of life's unavoidable pain.**

3. *Others are evangelized.* **As people notice the quality of life available to the children of God, some will desire to know Jesus because of what they see of Him in our lives.**

THINKING BACK

God wants to have a personal relationship with us. Our faith in Him establishes this relationship.

Revelation: He has given us His word, the Bible.

Faith: The Bible asks us to do some things against our natural inclinations. If we trust God and believe in Him, we do them. If we don't trust, we don't obey.

Blessing: If we believe God, and wholeheartedly obey the Bible, He blesses us with spiritual abundance.

Reproduction: If our lives exhibit the spiritual abundance of God, others will want to become Christians too.

SPEED BUMP!

1. **What is God's strategy for relating to humanity?**
Four main elements comprise God's strategy for relating to humanity: revelation, faith, blessing, and reproduction.

2. **How was God's strategy for relating to humanity executed in the Old Testament?**
God worked through the nation of Israel, promising earthly reward for trusting obedience.

3. **How was God's strategy for relating to humanity executed in the New Testament?**
God worked through the church, promising spiritual reward for trusting obedience.

4. **What are the consequences of faithful obedience to God?**
Our faithful obedience to God results in God's glory, our blessing, and a witness to the world.

FOR FURTHER STUDY

Scripture Passages

- Deuteronomy 28
- Psalm 67
- John 17:20-21
- Romans 15:4
- Romans 16:27
- 1 Corinthians 10:11
- Galatians 5:22-23

FAQ #29

 How Is the Bible Like a Mirror?

 The Bible is like a mirror in that it accurately reflects our spiritual appearance.

In *Snow White and the Seven Dwarfs,* the wicked queen asks her enchanted mirror, "Mirror, mirror on the wall, who's the fairest one of all?" The mirror cannot lie. So for years it says, "You, O queen, are the fairest in the land." But one day the mirror responds, "Snow White is the fairest of them all." The enraged queen decides to destroy Snow White. The plan fails, however. A handsome prince rescues Snow White and carries her away to live happily ever after.

Although only a fairy tale, the story is based on one fundamental truth. A mirror doesn't lie. If your nose is dirty, it tells you. If your hair is a mess, it tells you. If your clothes don't fit, it tells you. Anything about your appearance that you want to know, you can ask a mirror. It will tell you the truth every time.

In James 1:22-25 we read:

But prove yourselves doers of the word, and not merely hearers who delude themselves. For if any one is a hearer of the word and not a doer, he is like a man who looks at his natural face in a mirror; for once he has looked at himself and gone away, he has immediately forgotten what kind of person he was. But one who looks intently at the perfect law, the law of liberty, and abides by it, not having become a forgetful hearer but an effectual doer, this man shall be blessed in what he does (NASB).

> Scripture is like a pair of spectacles which dispels the darkness and gives us a clear view of God.
>
> *John Calvin*

When we look into the word of God, we see what we look like and are admonished to correct anything that is out of place. It discloses attitudes that need adjustment. It tells us if our values are a mess. It bares our dirty thoughts. And just as we correct what we see wrong in a glass mirror, so we must, by the guidance and strength of the Holy Spirit, correct the defects the spiritual mirror reveals.

Perhaps we have been harboring resentment over a fellow worker who received the promotion and raise we had hoped for. We look into the mirror, and we read, "Love does not envy" (1 Corinthians 13:4). Uh-oh. Later we read: "Bondservants [employees], obey in all things your masters [employers] according to the flesh, not with eyeservice, as men-pleasers, but in sincerity of heart, fearing God. And whatever you do, do it heartily, as to the Lord and not to men, knowing that from the Lord you will receive the reward of the inheritance; for you serve the Lord Christ" (Colossians 3:22-24). Ohhhh. The killer blow! Our attitude falls short of the word. We have no right to fume. We must give up the resentment.

The Bible as a mirror never lies.

Or, perhaps we are reliving our childhood through our child or children. We think that if we had received more guidance as a child we would have achieved great things. So we will make sure that our child accomplishes what we never did. We drive our child to succeed. Our child must attain the honor roll like our neighbor's child. Our child must excel in athletics like our brother's child. Our child has to play the piano well, like our preacher's child. Our child should be good-looking like our fellow committee member's child. We try not to show it, but we are disappointed when it isn't true. We cause our child to feel loved conditionally, that he or she can never please us.

Then we read, "Fathers [parents], do not provoke your children, lest they become discouraged" (Colossians 3:21); "do not provoke your children to wrath, but bring them up in the training and admonition of the Lord" (Ephesians 6:4); "train up a child in the way he should go, and when he is old he will not depart from it" (Proverbs 22:6).

Whoops! Our values are askew. They are a mess, and need to be cleaned up. We are exasperating our children, and they are becoming discouraged. We need to repent and line up our values according to God's word.

Or maybe we have gotten careless in watching television and going to movies. "After all," we say, "if we are going to let some common swearing, a little skin, or a bit of violence keep us from watching something, there won't be much to watch. Besides, that stuff doesn't affect me. I already have my values formed. I don't agree with the language, the skin, and the violence, so I just mentally screen it out."

Then we read, "I will walk within my house in the integrity of my heart. I will set no worthless thing before my eyes" (Psalm 101:2-3 NASB). And "do not participate in the unfruitful deeds of darkness, but instead even expose them; for it is disgraceful even to speak of the things which are done by them in secret" (Ephesians 5:11-12 NASB). Then again, "Finally, brethren, whatever is true, whatever is honorable, whatever is right, whatever is pure, whatever is lovely, whatever is of good repute, if there is any excellence and if anything worthy of praise, let your mind dwell on these things" (Philippians 4:8 NASB).

Hmmmm. Well, what we've been watching won't do. Our thoughts are soiled. They are vicarious thoughts, but they are soiled and need to be cleaned up.

The mirror doesn't lie. We can live in denial and go away without heeding the word, but then we become the person who sees a dirty nose, ratty hair, and ill-fitting clothes yet does nothing about it, forgetting what he really looks like.

FAQ #30

 How Is the Bible Like a Sword?

 The Bible is like a sword in that it can be used as a weapon both to defend us and attack the enemy.

I will never forget seeing a karate expert give a demonstration of his skill. After breaking boards with his hands and cement blocks with his head, he asked for a volunteer from the audience. (Why would anyone volunteer for anything at a karate demonstration?) He had the volunteer (a macho teenage boy) lie down on his back, and the expert laid a watermelon on the boy's stomach. Then the karate expert took out a sword sharp enough to shave a thirteen-year-old's peach fuzz. This three-and-a-half-foot long broadsword gleamed spotlessly in the midday sun before bleachers full of anxious spectators. The powerfully built wielder of this death-instrument raised it over his head with both hands. The only things between the boy and the blade was a plump watermelon and a T-shirt. The crowd held its breath. The sword flashed downward at a speed that would be missed if the eye blinked at the wrong moment. In a wink, it pierced the top of the melon rind, sliced through the red pulp, split the bottom of the melon rind, and stopped precisely where melon met T-shirt. The two cleanly split halves of the watermelon dropped neatly to the floor. The young man got up with a humble, sheepish grin on his face that said, "If I had known what I was getting into, I would never have volunteered."

It was an astonishing display of precision. One inch too short, and the watermelon would not have been cut in half. One inch too far, and the teenager would have been disemboweled. A fifth-degree black belt in karate is trained to kill, if need be, with skill, precision, effectiveness, and safety to himself. If he is trained to use a sword, he knows how to wield it on a level that an untrained person cannot even imagine.

This gives us additional insight to a passage such as Hebrews 4:12, which reads:

For the word of God is living and powerful, and sharper than any two-edged sword, piercing even to the division of soul and spirit, and of joints and marrow, and is a discerner of the thoughts and intents of the heart.

Just as a skilled swordsman is able to place his sword into a person's body at the exact point he chooses, so the word of God is able to pierce a person's soul and spirit at whatever precise point God elects.

Of course, the Holy Spirit applies the word of God to our needs. We read in 1 Corinthians 2:9-10, 12:

"Eye has not seen, nor ear heard, nor have entered into the heart of man, the things which God has prepared for those who love Him." But God has revealed them to us through His spirit. For the Spirit searches all things, yes, the deep things of God... Now we have received, not the spirit of the world, but the Spirit who is from God, that we might know the things that have been freely given to us by God.

When we struggle through a trial or flounder under some weakness, the Holy Spirit directs the word of God to us in a way that cuts directly to the issue. Are you struggling with worry? The Holy Spirit will take a passage like Matthew 6 and cause it to jump up off of the page:

Why I Need to Know This

In knowing this I will more fully comprehend the richness of the Bible and the many ways I can apply it to my daily life. In understanding the word pictures used to describe the Bible, I can now read the Bible and use it as a mirror to show me what I am really like, or as a sword to protect myself, or as light to illuminate my way, or as water to quench my spiritual thirst for answers to life's great questions, or as food for spiritual growth.

Which of you by worrying can add one cubit to his stature? Therefore do not worry, saying, "What shall we eat?" or "What shall we drink?" or "What shall we wear?" For after all these things the Gentiles seek. For your heavenly Father knows that you need all these things. But seek first the kingdom of God and His righteousness, and all these things shall be added to you. Therefore, do not worry about tomorrow, for tomorrow will worry about its own things. Sufficient for the day is its own trouble (vv. 27, 31-34).

If you are floundering under a weakness, the Holy Spirit will bring a passage alive to you, such as 1 Corinthians 9:24-27:

Do you not know that those who run in a race all run, but only one receives the prize? Run in such a way that you may win. And everyone who competes in the games exercises self-control in all things. They then do it to receive a perishable wreath, but we an imperishable. Therefore I run in such a way, as not without aim; I box in such a way, as not beating the air; but I buffet my body and make it my slave, lest possibly, after I have preached to others, I myself should be disqualified (NASB).

As the Holy Spirit uses the word of God, so can we. We play it for both defense and protection. We brandish it in attack when we advance into enemy territory. Ephesians 6:17 calls the word of God the "sword of the Spirit," part of the spiritual armor described in that chapter, which protects us from the wiles of the devil, and enables us to stand firm against him.

Jesus thwarted Satan with the word. After fasting forty days, Jesus was hungry. The devil urged Him to turn stones into bread, which, for reasons that are not fully explained, would have been wrong. Jesus' reply was, "It is written, 'Man shall not live by bread alone, but by every word that proceeds from the mouth of God.'" The devil then goaded Jesus to perform a flamboyant miracle to prove He was the Son of God. Jesus replied, "It is written again, 'You shall not tempt the Lord your God.'" Finally, the devil offered to give Jesus all the kingdoms of the world if Jesus would worship him. Jesus said, "Away with you, Satan! For it is written, 'You shall worship the Lord your God, and Him only you shall serve.'" Then the devil left Him (see Matthew 4:1-11).

The Spirit applies the sword with pinpoint accuracy to our pressing need.

In each instance, Jesus routed the devil by quoting Scripture to him. In this way, Jesus withstood the temptations of the great deceiver and destroyer. I am persuaded that Jesus quoted these Scriptures, not out of His omniscience as God, but, because as a child, He had memorized these passages, just as you and I have to memorize passages if we are to use them in similar circumstances. If Jesus used memorized Scripture to withstand the attacks of the enemy shouldn't we deploy the same strategy?

FAQ #31

Q How Is the Bible Like Light?

A The Bible is like light in that it enables us to see in the darkness of life so that we stay on the right path and avoid harm.

One of the wackier things I have done in my life is explore caves. I'm not particularly interested in exploring caves, but a friend of mine suggested it, and in a moment of shortsightedness, I agreed. We were living in Atlanta at the time, and we drove to a little-known spot where Alabama, Georgia, and Tennessee meet, called Lymrock Blowing Cave. From a "blowing" cave, a great rush of fifty-five-degree air blows out twenty-four hours a day. To keep us from opening our skulls on the sharp top of the cave when we came to low spots, we wore miner's helmets—hard hats with little lights on the top of them. The lights, of course, were to help us see. It seems a remote cave lacks electricity.

A river flowed through this cave, and after walking upstream in the river, we came to a fork in the cave. Several forks later found us walking on solid ground. Since my friend had made this trip several times before, I trusted him to know where we were going. Finally, the cave narrowed so that we had to squeeze ourselves through some passages. In fact, one spot was so narrow that I had to exhale and force myself through the passage into a larger space before I could inhale again. It is one of those things to brag about now, but you could never get me to do again in a million years!

One thing that bothered me was the possibility of losing our light, even though we had our miner's helmets, a flashlight apiece, and plenty of batteries. We turned off our lights just to see what it would be like. Involuntarily, my eyelids reached for the ceiling and my eyes bugged like a bullfrog's. The total absence of light a half a mile back into a room in a cave that you had to squeeze yourself into is a level of darkness that I could not have comprehended without experiencing it. I put my hand in front of my eyes and waved it around to see if I could detect any motion. I couldn't. Then we turned our lights back on and walked out of the cave.

The Scriptures are a miner's helmet, a flashlight in a dark cave.

The lights on our helmets were surprisingly weak. (The weaker the bulb, the longer the battery will last.) It didn't take much light to get out of the cave. But without the light, I am sure my bones would still be in that cave. No way in the world would we ever have gotten out of the cave without light. When you cannot see, you are an absolute victim to your surroundings. You don't know the turns, the holes, the breaks in the rock that lead you from room to room. Without light, you are lost, doomed to flounder and stumble, imprisoned by the elements, and destined to die in the darkness.

This experience gave new meaning to the passages, "The entrance of Your words gives light;" and "Your word is a lamp to my feet, and a light to my path" (Psalm 119:130, 105). The metaphor is clear. Ignorance of the word and ignorance of the truth is darkness as black as the cave I visited. The Scriptures are a miner's helmet—a flashlight. A modern paraphrase of this passage might be, "Your word is a miner's helmet to my feet, and a flashlight to my path."

Without the Scriptures, we are victims of our surroundings. We don't know where to walk in life. We don't know which passages lead us to safety. We cannot see the pitfalls, the cliffs, or the low headroom. We don't know when to turn right or when to turn left. We cannot even walk straight, because without sight to guide us, we wander in circles.

The Scriptures help us see, and lead us to safety. If we will learn the Bible and commit ourselves to following it, then it is light to us in a dark world.

FAQ #32

 How Is the Bible Like Water?

 The Bible is like water in that it quenches our thirst and cleanses us from spiritual impurities.

I know what it is like to be thirsty. I spent my summers in high school on the farm baling hay, and later worked my way through college on summer construction jobs that had me toiling on hot pavement, or on metal roofs, or in holes with a pick and shovel. I would get so thirsty that I thought I would have to duct-tape a water hose to my mouth to quench it. One hot July day, with the temperature nearing 100 degrees, I was baling hay. Working without a shirt on, my body became slick with sweat. As I hiked the last bale onto the wagon high over my head, the chaff from the hay rained down on me like salt from a shaker that pours too fast. It covered me with itchy bits of alfalfa, some of which lodged between my belt and my skin. I was so thirsty, I thought I would die. Visions of a lost soul crawling across an endless, mirage-filled desert danced in my mind. There and then, I decided to go to college and graduate school for as long as I needed, in order to get a job in an air-conditioned office in the summertime.

God's word slakes our spiritual thirst.

People who have been shipwrecked have been known to go insane because of thirst. The internal drive for water when the body needs it is intense.

I also know what it means to be spiritually thirsty. We thirst for meaning and purpose, to know who we are and why we are here, to know where we came from and where we are going. We thirst for meaningful relationships. And when we have wandered without sense and purpose, when we have gone too long without the answers to life's great questions, we develop a driving thirst that must be satisfied or our soul shrivels and dies.

During a time of intense spiritual thirst, I came to Christ, Who is the Living Word of God (John 1:1, 14; Revelation 19:13). I had been longing for purpose and meaning, yearning to know what life was all about, and hoping for some assurance for life after death. My thirst drove me to seek God, and He gave me "living water" so that I would never have to thirst again. I learned who I was (a child of God), where I had come from (created by Him), why I was here (to know Him and make Him known), and where I was going (to live with God in heaven forever). Such wonderful news was like a tall glass of cool, pure water on a sweltering summer day. It soothed my parched throat, slaked my thirst, and poured life into my soul.

The "living water" image comes from the Gospel of John, chapter four, in which Jesus is talking with a woman at a Samaritan well in the heat of the day. He asked the woman if she would give him a drink of water. She wondered why Jesus, a Jew, would speak to a Samaritan, since there was historic hatred between Jews and Samaritans. Jesus said, "If you knew who you were talking to, you would ask Him and He would give you living water, and never thirst again." The woman found the living water that afternoon, and never thirsted again. In that way, the word of God is like water.

The word is also like water in that it cleanses us. We read in Ephesians 5:25-26, "Husbands, love your wives, just as Christ also loved the church and gave Himself for her, that He might sanctify and cleanse her with the washing of water by the word." And we read in 1 John 1:8-9, "If we say that we have no sin, we deceive ourselves, and the truth is not in us. If we confess our sins, He is faithful and just to forgive us our sins and to cleanse us from all unrighteousness."

The word, as a mirror, shows us where the dirt (sin) is in our lives, and then the same word, as water, cleanses us as we confess our sins. Life and cleansing, two wonderful gifts of the word, are ways in which the word is like water.

FAQ #33

 How Is the Bible Like Food?

 The Bible is like food in that it satisfies our spiritual hunger, and enables us to grow.

When I was working construction in college, not only did I get very thirsty, I also got ravenously hungry. Hard work revved up an already rapid metabolism to turbocharged speed. For breakfast, I ate three eggs, a half-dozen slices of bacon, four pieces of toast, a large glass of orange juice, and a big bowl or two of cereal. For lunch, which I carried in an ice chest instead of a lunch box, I ate two big lunchmeat or meatloaf sandwiches, a sixteen-ounce can of pears, peaches, or applesauce, a quart of milk and several packages of

Twinkies, Ding-Dongs, or other such delicacies. My appetite astonished even me. Half an hour after eating a huge supper, I would saunter into the living room with a sixteen-ounce glass of milk and half a loaf of bread made up into peanut butter and jelly sandwiches. My mother still comments on that today. One of the great sources of relief in my adult life is that I don't have to feed anyone who eats like that.

Hunger is a driving force, and it demands to be filled just as does thirst. To satisfy that hunger, Jesus the Word of God offers Himself to us again, this time as the Bread of Life:

Jesus answered them and said, "Truly, truly, I say to you, you seek Me, not because you saw signs, but because you ate of the loaves, and were filled. Do not work for the food which perishes, but for the food which endures to eternal life, which the Son of Man shall give to you, for on Him the Father, even God, has set His seal."

They said therefore to Him, "What shall we do, that we may work the works of God?"
Jesus answered and said to them, "This is the work of God, that you believe in Him whom He has sent."
They said therefore to Him, "What then do You do for a sign, that we may see, and believe You? What work do You perform? Our fathers ate the manna in the wilderness; as it is written, 'He gave them bread out of heaven to eat.'"

Jesus therefore said to them, "Truly, truly, I say to you, it is not Moses who has given you the bread out of heaven, but it is My Father who gives you the true bread out of heaven. For the bread of God is that which comes down out of heaven, and gives life to the world."

They said therefore to Him, "Lord, evermore give us this bread."

Jesus said to them, "I am the bread of life; he who comes to Me shall not hunger, and he who believes in Me shall never thirst" (John 6:26-35 NASB).

The word is also called milk. Peter writes, "as newborn babes, desire the pure milk of the word, that you may grow thereby" (1 Peter 2:2 NASB).

The writer of the Book of Hebrews writes:

The word of God nourishes eternal life and abundant life.

For though by this time you ought to be teachers, you have need again for someone to teach you the elementary principles of the oracles of God, and you have come to need milk and not solid food. For everyone who partakes only of milk is not accustomed to the word of righteousness, for he is a babe. But solid food is for the mature, who because of practice have their senses trained to discern good and evil (Hebrews 5:12-14 NASB).

The Word of God gives us eternal life as well as abundant life. Jesus said, "I have come that they may have life, and that they may have it more abundantly" (John 10:10 NASB). The word sustains us, strengthens us, and encourages growth. It is the spiritual source of all that gives us life. In that way, the word of God has been pictured as food.

THINKING BACK

Both Jesus—the Living Word of God—and the Bible—the written word of God—are sources of life, providing the reflection of truth, the weapons of defense, light in darkness, water for our thirst, and food for our hunger.

SPEED BUMP!

1. How is the Bible like a mirror?
The Bible is like a mirror in that it accurately reflects our spiritual appearance.

2. How is the Bible like a sword?
The Bible is like a sword in that it can be used as a weapon both to defend us and attack the enemy.

3. How is the Bible like light?
The Bible is like light in that it enables us to see in the darkness of life so that we stay on the right path and avoid harm.

4. How is the Bible like water?
The Bible is like water in that it quenches our thirst and cleanses us from spiritual impurities.

5. How is the Bible like food?
The Bible is like food in that it satisfies our spiritual hunger, and enables us to grow.

FOR FURTHER STUDY

Scripture Passages

- Psalm 119:130
- Matthew 4:1-11
- John 6:26-35
- Ephesians 5:25-26
- Ephesians 6:17
- Hebrews 4:12
- James 1:22-25

FAQ #34

 What Is the Foundation for Bible Study?

 The foundation for Bible study is spiritual rebirth, a desire to know the Bible, an obedient heart, and a plan to learn.

First, we have already seen in 1 Corinthians 2:14 that "the natural man (the non-Christian) does not receive the things of the Spirit of God, for they are foolishness to him; nor can he know them, because they are spiritually discerned." If a person isn't a Christian, he cannot grasp the spiritual truths of the Scripture. He can learn all about people, places, and events, but grasping the spiritual truths behind them and being changed by them is beyond him.

Second, the person must want to learn the Bible. The Bible claims to be the source of truth for living acceptably before God, and for ultimate meaning in life. God promises, to the person who walks in the spirit, the fruit of the Spirit: love, joy, peace, and more. If you had those three things, would you want anything else? What else is there?

The question we must ask ourselves is, "Do we believe it?" We may say we believe many things, but our actions betray us. If we believed them, we would act differently. By not studying the Bible, we indicate that we believe there is another avenue for a meaningful life. In fact, some of us have tried studying the Bible, and it was so hard, so boring, or so unyielding of anything significant, that life is easier not studying so hard. However, the question still comes back, do we believe the

> Disregard the study of God and you sentence yourself to stumble and blunder through life, blindfolded, as it were, with no sense of direction and no understanding of what surrounds you.
>
> *J. I. Packer*

Bible? If we do, we have to believe that life can be lived more fully by being mature in the Scriptures than by being immature in the Scriptures. We must not allow ourselves the hypocritical position of saying that we believe the Bible to be the source of ultimate meaning in life, and then fail to study it.

Third, the person must cultivate obedience. If we decide to believe the Bible, then at some point in our life we must commit ourselves to seriously studying it. Three very crucial tests of a Christian's commitment face a person after accepting Jesus. The first is, when the Christian life becomes harder than one first thought it was going to be, "Am I going to commit myself totally to following Jesus, or am I going to do it half-heartedly?" The second one is, "Am I going to accept the Great Commission (Jesus' command to take the message of salvation by grace through faith in Christ to the whole world-Matthew 28:19-20) as my own personal commission, and do what I can to further it?" The third one is, "Am I going to become a serious student of the Bible?" Unless we face these three tests squarely and answer yes to each, we usually play around at Christianity.

> **S**uccess in Bible study takes time and effort.

Fourth in the foundation is developing a plan to learn the Bible. Most of us work hard to gain the knowledge and skills we need for success in careers, personal relationships, or various sports or hobbies. Success at anything worthwhile takes time and effort. We should not be surprised that the spiritual realm is no different. In fact, Paul urged Timothy: "Ttrain yourself to be godly. For physical training is of some value, but godliness has value for all things, holding promise for both the present life and the life to come" (1 Timothy 4:7-8 NIV). Learning the Bible well is no easier than getting in excellent physical shape. But in the end, the rewards are greater.

So what's our method? We can't join a Bible spa and work out every night after work. So what can we do? What method do we use? A method involves specific steps taken in a prescribed order to reach a definite goal.

FAQ #35

 What Are the Three Keys to Bible Study?

 The three keys to Bible study are observation, interpretation, and application.

Observation of the text comes first. The key question here is "What does it say?" You immerse yourself in the text. Like a good detective, you note and list the details and relationships you see for further thought and comparison.

The second step is interpretation. At this point you attempt to answer the question "What does it mean?" The student tries to determine the author's purpose, thoughts, attitudes, and emotions. How would the original recipients have understood the message?

The final step is application. The pertinent question is "What does it mean to me?" In other words, how should my life change as a result of what God says in this passage? As Howard Hendricks said, "The Bible was not given to make us more intelligent sinners, but to change our lives." The Bible is the Word of God; as such, it demands an obedient and appropriate response.

Why I Need to Know This

If I don't realize that spiritual rebirth is a prerequisite for really understanding the Bible, I may try to study the Bible without being a Christian, and become frustrated at its seeming lack of significance. If I don't know the fundamentals of observation, then even if I am a Christian, I am liable to be clumsy and ineffective in my attempts to study the Bible.

FAQ #36

Why Is Observation of the Bible So Important?

Observation is important, because unless we have observed correctly, we do not have reliable information.

Some people feel that observation wastes time. However, Oletta Wald asserts:

The first skill you need to develop is to train your mind to see when you read a passage—to observe carefully the words, to be on the alert for details. Too many of us are in the habit of reading Scripture without seeing very much, without thinking about the words we are seeing. We read words, but we do not observe what the words are saying. Sometimes we do not even see all the words in a passage. We are lazy observers! Because of inaccurate and careless observations, we often make faulty interpretations and shallow applications *(The Joy of Discovery in Bible Study,* revised edition, p. 16).

Howard Hendricks, who has taught personal Bible study to seminary students for over forty years, comments:

Observation will give you the basic building blocks out of which you will construct the meaning of a passage. The answers to your questions will come directly from the observation process. That is why I say, the more time you spend in Observation, the less time you will need to spend in Interpretation, and the more accurate will be your results. The less time you spend in Observation, the more time you will need to spend in Interpretation, and the less accurate will be your results *(Living by the Book,* p. 39).

The task of the observer is detection. If Sherlock Holmes had not been a careful observer, he wouldn't have solved a single case. He unraveled mysteries by seeing things others didn't see. He noticed small details missed by others, then drew inferences which cracked the case.

Studying the Bible is much the same. Although all Scripture is inspired of God and beneficial to us (2 Timothy 3:15-16), in one sense we are "reading someone else's mail." Each book of the Bible was written over 1,900 years ago in one or more non-English languages to address specific situations and questions. We lack a firsthand acquaintance with the authors and the recipients. So when studying a particular text we need to accurately and fully notice the details, discerning what is important and what is not.

Careful observation lays the foundation for good Bible study.

Careful observation requires the purpose, patience, and diligence illustrated in a New York Times advertisement for Mortimer Adler's *How to Read a Book.* Beneath the picture of a perplexed teenager poring over a letter were these words:

HOW TO READ A LOVE LETTER

This young man has just received his first love letter. He may have read it three or four times, but he is just beginning. To read it as accurately as he would like would require several dictionaries and a good deal of close work with a few experts of etymology and philology.

However, he will do all right without them.

He will ponder over the exact shade of meaning of every word, every comma. She has headed the letter, "Dear John." What, he asks himself, is the exact significance of these words? Did she refrain from saying "Dearest" because she was bashful? Would "My Dear" have sounded too formal?

Jeepers, maybe she would have said "Dear So-and-So" to anybody!

A worried frown will now appear on his face. But it disappears as soon as he really gets to thinking about the first sentence. She certainly wouldn't have written that to anybody!

And so he works his way through the letter, one moment perched blissfully on a cloud, the next moment huddled miserably behind an eight-ball. It has started a hundred questions in his mind. He could quote it by heart. In fact, he will—to himself for weeks to come (quoted in Robert A. Traina, *Methodical Bible Study*, pp. 97-98).

The advertisement concluded, "If people read books with anything like the same concentration, we'd be a race of mental giants." And if Christians read the Bible, God's love letter to us, with the same concentration, we would be a race of spiritual giants.

FAQ #37

How Can We Observe the Bible?

We observe the Bible by developing a strategy that forces us to look closely at the text.

Years ago, Yogi Berra was a catcher with the world champion New York Yankees. Three times Most Valuable Player in the league, he later became a manager and led the Yankees to the World Series Championship. He is in the Baseball Hall of Fame, and everyone agrees that he is a baseball genius. But if there were also a malapropism hall of fame, he would be a charter member. Don't know what a malapropism is? Listen: (speaking of the game of baseball, Yogi said) "Ninety percent of this game is half mental!" That's a malapropism (a comical confusion of words)! And his brain was either wired or unwired to be able to fire these things off at the speed of speech:

- **A nickel ain't worth a dime anymore.**
- **Mickey Mantle's (one of baseball's greatest hitters) a switch hitter because he's amphibious.**
- **Slump? I ain't in no slump. I just ain't hitting.**
- **You give a hundred percent in the first half of the game, and if it isn't enough, in the second half, you give what's left.**
- **You got to be careful if you don't know where you're going, because you might not get there.**
- **What makes a great baseball manager, you ask? The answer is, a great baseball team!**

Oh, Yogi! How do you do it?

I brought all this up because he said something else useful to us now: "You can see a lot just by looking." Ain't it the truth? In his own garbled way, he's talking about the need to observe carefully. You really can see a lot if you just look carefully.

To start your observations, get a pencil and paper. Because you would otherwise remember only a small number of your observations, write them down, whether in your study Bible, in a notebook, or in your computer. To get an idea of the overall picture, first read the book through in its entirety. For beginners, you might want to pick a smaller book (three to five chapters is a good size).

Use the Six Basic Questions

Rudyard Kipling once wrote,

**I keep six honest serving men
(They taught me all I knew);**

**Their names are What and Why and When
And How and Where and Who.**

When determining what to observe, the six basic questions are always helpful.

Who is the author? To whom is he writing? List all the people involved. List anything that strikes you about a character.

What happened and in what order? What ideas are presented?

Where did this take place? What are the characteristics of the geographic setting? Where are the recipients? (Study with a map and every time a place is mentioned, look it up on the map.) Information will come alive if you do this!

When did the events in the text take place? When did they occur in relation to other events in Scripture and in secular history? When was the writer writing? You may need a Bible history book in order to answer these questions.

Focus your observation with the six basic questions.

Why does a particular person do or say something? Why is a particular "teaching" presented?

How are things accomplished? How well? By what method?

Note Key Terms

Look for key *terms*, those words that seem most important for understanding the passage. Repetition of a term, phrase, or clause is often a good clue as to what the author is attempting to communicate. For example, the word "believe" appears 79 times in John's Gospel and is critical to an understanding of its message. In fact, John asserts that his purpose in recording certain miraculous signs was "that you may believe that Jesus is the Christ, the Son of God, and that believing you may have life in His name" (John 20:31). Similarly, the repetition of "do not worry" or "do not be anxious" gives a strong indication as to Jesus' thrust in Matthew 6:25-34. One cannot understand Paul's excellent summary of the gospel message in Romans 3:21-26 apart from such terms as "law," "the Law," "righteousness," "faith," "sin," "grace," "justify," "redemption," and "sacrifice of atonement."

Identify the Structure

Hendricks and Hendricks suggest the student look for five different kinds of literary structure (The following is summarized from *Living By the Book,* pp. 118-119).

Authors of narratives frequently use biographical structure as they focus on key individuals in their stories. For example, Genesis 12-50 shifts the spotlight in turn to four generations of family leaders: Abraham, Isaac, Jacob, and Joseph. The Book of Judges is structured around the various leaders known as judges who God raised up during the period between Joshua and Samuel.

A book's structure tells you how its parts merge to accomplish its purpose.

In geographical structure the focus is on place. To understand the structure of Exodus the reader must note the various places that the nation of Israel visits as it travels from Egypt to the Promised Land.

Historical structure is based on the key events. The Book of Joshua is built upon the reporting of different events. The Lord commissions Joshua to lead the people into the Promised Land after the death of Moses. Spies are sent out for reconnaissance. Israel crosses the Jordan. Jericho falls. Due to Achan's sin the Israelites initially experience defeat at Ai. And so on as they conquer the land.

Chronological structure, emphasizing key times, is closely related to historical structure. Narratives usually proceed in this way. The temporal progression of events is often signaled by connectives such as "after," "before," "meanwhile," "now," "since," "then," "until," "when," "whenever," and "while."

Ideological structure is organized around key ideas and concepts. Most of the epistles are developed in this way. Once you determine the central purpose, it is relatively easy to outline the book because you can see how each part contributes to that purpose. For example, many of the books of the New Testament begin with the presentation of spiritual and doctrinal truth. The rest of the book talks about how our lives should be changed by that truth.

The first three chapters of Ephesians are spent talking about how God has provided a way for us to be saved from our sins through Christ, and that this salvation is by grace through faith in Him. The last three chapters are spent talking about how the Ephesian believers ought to be living in light of the things that God has already done for them. The transition from one part to the other is Ephesians 4:1, which says, "I, therefore, the prisoner of the Lord, beseech you to walk worthy of the calling with which you were called." In the first three chapters, Paul explained "the calling" with which they were called. Then, he says, "live worthy of your calling."

Structural relationships or patterns help you understand a passage. Note the use of comparisons and contrasts. *Comparisons* show how things are alike. Connectives used to indicate comparisons include "also," "as," "even so," "just as…so," "like," "likewise," and "too." For example, in James 3:3-5 the tongue is compared to the bit in a horse's mouth, a ship rudder, and a spark that starts a forest fire. *Contrasts* show how things differ. Sample connectives include "although," "but," "however," "much more," "nevertheless," and "yet." Galatians 5:19-23 contrasts the deeds of the flesh with the fruit of the Spirit.

The potential importance of *repetition* has been alluded to earlier in the discussion of key terms. Authors can also signal what is important to them by repeating characters, circumstances, patterns, and other Scripture. Be alert to *proportion*, which indicates the importance of something by the amount of space the author devotes to different subjects or periods of time. For example, Genesis devotes only eleven chapters to the comparatively lengthy period from creation to Abraham and thirty-nine chapters to Abraham and the next three generations of his family (Isaac, Jacob, and Joseph). This coverage signals the author's narrowed focus on the family God chose to be His instrument of blessing to all peoples (Genesis 12:1-3).

Identify the Literary Form

Determining literary form is important in reading any piece of literature. There are several kinds of literature in the Bible. Historical books tell stories. Poetical books give us poetry and song. Prophetical books foretell the future and speak God's will forcefully. Epistles, which are letters to churches or individuals, instruct us in practical daily living based on biblical truth.

You will not see the things in poetry that you do in history. In history the "who, what, why, when, where, and how" are expressed in a sequence that the writer believes will help the audience see the points the writer wants to make, which usually focus on explaining divine and human action. Those questions usually aren't expressed or answered in the same way as poetry. So be aware that some methods of observation work better on some kinds of literature in the Bible than they do on others. Description of the different kinds of literature and the special interpretive principles for each are described in the next chapter.

Observe the Atmosphere

Observe the general tone of a passage. Is the mood joyful, sorrowful, thankful, concerned, angry, despairing? The author's words and setting shed light on the atmosphere. Paul's emphasis in Philippians on being joyful takes on added impact when one realizes he was writing from a Roman prison.

These basic principles of observation will help get you started. The important thing is to start studying the Bible and making whatever observations you can, asking as many questions as you can. When you know what questions to ask, the answers are often very rewarding.

SPEED BUMP!

1. **What is the foundation for Bible study?**
The foundation for Bible study is spiritual rebirth, a desire to know the Bible, an obedient heart, and a plan to learn.

2. **What are the three keys to Bible study?**
The three keys to Bible study are observation, interpretation, and application.

3. **Why is observation of the Bible so important?**
Observation is important, because unless we have observed correctly, we do not have reliable information.

4. How can we observe the Bible?

We observe the Bible by developing a strategy that forces us to look closely at the text.

FAQ #38

 Why Is Interpretation Necessary?

 Interpretation is necessary because it is not always clear to us what a biblical writer meant by what he wrote.

From time to time one hears the protest, "Why do you have to interpret the Bible? Just read it and do what it says!" At one level, it is easy to understand and sympathize with this sentiment. The meaning of many biblical passages does seem straightforward. Furthermore, for most of us, our major problem with the Bible is not the parts that we don't understand but with the parts that we do—that is, in obeying such commands as "Do not repay evil for evil" (Romans 12:17) or "Be joyful in hope, patient in affliction, faithful in prayer" (Romans 12:12 NIV).

Other passages are not so straightforward. For example, when we read an English version of the Bible, we are already involved in interpretation. The final clause of 1 Corinthians 7:1 has been translated in varied ways such as: (a) "It is good for a man not to touch a woman" (KJV); (b) "It is a good principle for a man to have no physical contact with women" (PHILLIPS); (c) "It is a good thing for a man to have nothing to do with women" (NEB); (d) "It is good for a man not to marry" (NIV); and (e) "It is a good thing for

> If you believe what you like in the Gospel and reject what you do not like, it is not the Gospel you believe, but yourself.
>
> *St. Augustine*

a man not to touch a woman" (NAB). Note the NIV footnote, "It is good for a man not to have sexual relations with a woman," which expresses the ancient idiom "to touch a woman." So interpretation by the translators has already begun, even before we pick up an English Bible.

Also, all of us then bring to the Bible our own knowledge, attitudes, and beliefs about God, religion, and "reality," which will influence the way in which we construe the meaning of a biblical text. For example, when we read the word "church" we often think of a particular type of building, despite the fact that a biblical meaning of "church" is "the community of people who have placed their faith in Christ" and the early church met in homes rather than in church buildings for the first three hundred years of its existence.

Not only is interpretation unavoidable, but different interpreters do not always agree. "Bible-believing Christians" disagree about such things as the mode of baptism, whether one can lose his or her salvation, and the nature of restrictions on the participation of women in the church. Some Christians assert that God's will for all Christians is material prosperity on the basis of texts such as 3 John 2, "Beloved, I wish above all things that thou mayest prosper and be in health" (KJV) [usually omitting the qualification "*even as thy soul prospereth*" (emphasis added)], a verse that has nothing to do with financial prosperity. Many cults misread and distort the meaning of various biblical passages.

However, as Gordon D. Fee and Douglas Stuart point out, "The antidote to bad interpretation is not no interpretation, but good interpretation based upon common-sense guidelines" (*How to Read the Bible for All Its Worth*, second edition, p. 17).

Interpretation is necessary not only because of who we are as readers but also because of the nature of Scripture itself. The Bible is the message of a changeless God and, as such, is timeless and always relevant. However, as Fee and Stuart explain, the Bible

The antidote to bad interpretation, is not no interpretation, but good interpretation.

is *not* a series of propositions and imperatives; it is not simply a collection of "Sayings from Chairman God," as though he looked down at us from heaven and said: "Hey you down there, learn these truths. Number 1, There is no God but One, and I am he. Number 2, I am the Creator of all things, including humankind"—and so on, all the way through proposition 7,777 and imperative 777 (emphasis theirs, p. 18).

> **The Bible is not a series of propositions and imperatives.**

Although the Bible does contain these truths, they are not recorded in this form. "Throughout the Bible God becomes personally involved in people's lives. He doesn't offer pious platitudes but rather speaks directly to their needs in ways that are appropriate to their situations," Jack Kuhatschek says in *Taking the Guesswork Out of Applying the Bible* (p. 29). God, through human authors, wrote the biblical texts to be timely to their original recipients. Therefore, the biblical texts address specific situations and questions. This historical particularity makes interpretation of the Bible challenging and fascinating.

The goal of Bible interpretation must be to understand what the author was trying to say to his original readers. As Gordon D. Fee and Douglas Stuart note, "God's Word to us was first of all his Word to them" (p. 18). They elaborate: "*A text cannot mean what it never*

Why I Need to Know This

If I don't understand that certain principles must be followed in the interpretation of Scripture, I am liable to draw wrong conclusions from what I read in the Bible. We cannot always know if we truly understand a difficult portion of Scripture, even with a proper understanding of the principles of interpretation. But without them, we can easily misunderstand even the simplest and most forthright passage.

meant. Or to put it in a positive way, the true meaning of the biblical text for us is what God originally intended it to mean when it was first spoken. This is the starting point" (p. 26). To understand what the Bible means, we must first understand what it meant to the original readers. This is hard, however, because of the distance of time, culture, and language between us and the first readers.

Time

The sixty-six books of the Bible were composed over a 1,500-year period that ended nineteen centuries ago. The world has changed a great deal since the last words were written. Without study we don't know what the world was like then. Without that knowledge, it is hard for us to understand what is at stake in many parts of the Bible. For example, it is hard to understand Jonah's unwillingness to obey God and preach in Nineveh until we learn that Nineveh was the most hated nation (and not just by Israel) of the eighth century B.C. It was a cross between Nazi Germany and the Mafia. Why should he want to help them?

A text cannot mean what it never meant.

Culture

Significant cultural distance separates us from the world of the biblical texts. For example, we cannot understand the Book of Ruth apart from understanding the right and responsibility an available relative had to redeem the land of his dead relative and raise up a child to the childless widow. Also, writers living before the discovery of germs or molecules did not express truth in the ways and manners of modern scientists. If they had, their writings would have made no sense to anyone until our age arrived.

Geography

We are also geographically distant from the authors and recipients of the biblical books.

A knowledge of geography is helpful in understanding a passage such as John 2:11-13, in which Jesus had just been to a wedding in the Galilean town of Cana:

This beginning of His signs Jesus did in Cana of Galilee, and manifested His glory, and His disciples believed in Him. After this He went down to Capernaum, He and His mother, and His brothers, and His disciples; and there they stayed a few days. And the Passover of the Jews was at hand, and Jesus went up to Jerusalem (NASB).

Why did John say they went down to Capernaum from Cana, when Capernaum is north of Cana? And why did he say they went up to Jerusalem when Jerusalem is south of Capernaum? The answer is that we, in the modern world, are oriented to looking at maps with north being up and south being down. If we are in Florida, we say we are going up to New York. If we are in Washington, we say we are going down to California. But the ancients of Bible times did not have maps the way we do. When they said they went down from Cana to Capernaum, they meant they went down! That is, they descended in altitude. Cana is in the hills. Capernaum is on the shore of the Sea of Galilee, lower in altitude than Cana. When they went up to Jerusalem from Capernaum, John meant they went up! Approximately a thousand feet! When you are walking, you are acutely aware of what up and down are (down is easier). Knowing the location of the towns, the approximate terrain, the major bodies of water, and so forth helps a person visualize these verses, and they come to life. Without a knowledge of geography, these verses tend to lie lifeless on the page.

The Bible teaches truth in the ways and manners of expressing truth in ancient times.

Language

Linguistic distance separates us from the biblical texts. The Old Testament was primarily written in ancient Hebrew, although there are a few passages in the related tongue of Aramaic. The New Testament was composed in Greek. The authors in each use words and phrases with which we are not totally familiar. As was pointed out earlier, the translation of the Scriptures into English itself requires interpretation.

Without the Holy Spirit's help, no one understands spiritual truth.

In order to communicate His message as clearly as possible, God used many different forms of literature, including formal instruction, narration, parables, poetry and proverbs, and prophecy. Each of these literary forms has special principles that must be followed for proper interpretation. Before we examine the various forms of literature and the specific principles for interpreting them, let us look at general principles of interpretation that will help us understand any portion of Scripture.

FAQ #39

 What Can Help Me Interpret the Scriptures?

 Certain principles of interpretation must be followed for any passage of Scripture.

As we said in the previous chapter on observation, spiritual rebirth, the illumination of the Holy Spirit, and an obedient heart are necessary to properly interpret the Bible. In 1 Corinthians 2:14 we read, "The man without the Spirit does not accept the things that come from the Spirit of God, for they are foolishness to him, and he cannot understand them because they are spiritually discerned" (NIV). This is not to say that non-Christians can understand nothing of the Bible's message, but they cannot understand its spiritual significance and be willing to obey the truth unless the Holy Spirit enlightens and convicts them. Even for Christians, diligent study, obedience, and submission to the truth of God's Word are necessary for spiritual understanding and insight (see Hebrews 5:12-14). As Walt Henrichsen summarizes in *A Layman's Guide to Interpreting the Bible:*

Seeing things from God's point of view is a ministry of the Holy Spirit to those who have not only trusted Him for salvation but for enlightenment as well. Though being a Christian is no guarantee that you will accurately interpret every passage in the Bible, it is foundational for properly understanding spiritual truth (p. 27).

The Holy Spirit enlightens us as we prayerfully seek His guidance while following sound procedures of interpretation.

Literary context

The meaning of any passage of Scripture will be consistent with what comes before and after the passage. "Context" is important for several reasons.

A. Berkeley Mickelsen in *Interpreting the Bible* summarizes the importance of context as follows:

Context is important because thought is usually expressed in a series of related ideas. Occasionally a person does make a swift and radical departure from the train of thought he is pursuing. Sometimes thoughts are tied together loosely by a general theme. But whether ideas are thus bound by close logical union or whether the main propositions are developed by repetition, the meaning of any particular element is nearly always controlled by what precedes and what follows (p. 100).

Honoring the contexts of a passage keeps us from twisting Scripture.

Too often we are guilty of "proof-texting," taking brief passages (often verses or portions of verses) out of context and quoting them in support of a doctrine or action. I will never forget, as a new Christian, how I used to take 1 Corinthians 2:9, "Eye has not seen, nor ear heard, nor have entered into the heart of man the things which God has prepared for those who love Him," and wax eloquent on the glories of heaven. My ears flamed with embarrassment when the next verse was pointed out to me: "But God has revealed them to us through His Spirit." So! The "wonderful things that God has prepared for those who love Him" are not referring to heaven at all, but the spiritual blessings we have now through the revelation of the Holy Spirit. I had been innocently guilty of taking the passage out of context and making it say something the author never intended it to say.

Here is another example. A Christian counselor reported that a woman he was counseling told him that God revealed to her that she was to divorce her husband and marry another man (with whom she was romantically involved) on the basis of Paul's exhortation in Ephesians 4:24, "Put on the new man" (KJV) (H. L. Bussell, *Unholy Devotions*, p. 119; cited in Klein, *et al.*, p. 7)! Give me a break! If we allow ourselves the freedom to take passages out of context, we can make the Bible say nearly anything we want it to say, even if it violently contradicts what the author originally meant.

Cults commonly cite verses out of context in order to claim biblical support for their erroneous beliefs and practices. Therefore, always make sure that the meaning of the passage you quote in support of a particular viewpoint has that meaning contextually. The smaller the passage you are studying, the greater is the likelihood of its being taken out of context. That is why the (modern) paragraph, which generally reflects a complete thought, is the basic unit of study.

Correct contextual interpretation of a passage involves examining:

- the immediate context;
- the book context;
- the context of other writings by the same author (if available);
- the context of the Testament you are studying (Old or New); and
- the entire Bible context.

The Bible will never contradict itself, either in the next paragraph, or in the previous paragraph.

The immediate context of a paragraph is usually the preceding two or three paragraphs and the subsequent two or three paragraphs. Chapter divisions are not inspired, and therefore are not always reliable boundary guides to immediate context, so don't be stopped by them when studying the context of a passage.

Three types of information from the context can help interpret a given passage correctly. Does the interpretation fit the stated or apparent purpose of the book? Does it fit the flow of thought in the book? Do parallel passages shed any light on the passage you are studying? A parallel passage is any passage elsewhere in the Bible which deals with the same subject you are studying.

Historical-cultural Background

All the books of the Bible were written in a specific time and a specific place by a specific person for specific people. If we are going to understand what was written, it is often helpful to know as much as we can about the historical and cultural background of the writing. For example, in the letter to the church at Laodicea (Revelation 3:14-22), Christ condemns it for being "neither cold nor hot" and goes on to state "I wish you were either one or the other." Klein; *et al.* explain that:

The smaller the passage, the more carefully you must examine its context.

We must interpret "hot" and "cold" in light of the historical context of Laodicea, which was located close to both hot springs (by Hierapolis) and a cold stream (by Colossae). Now both hot and cold water are desirable; both are useful for distinct purposes. But the spiritual state of this church more closely resembled the tepid lukewarm water that eventually flowed into Laodicean pipes. Neither hot nor cold, it was putrid and emetic (causing vomiting). Jesus is *not* saying that active opposition to him (an incorrect interpretation of "cold") is better than being a lukewarm Christian (pp. 175-176).

It is not enough to be aware of historical facts and the customs of the particular cultural setting(s); the interpreter must be aware of the impact that the message would have had on the original audience. A modern audience is not surprised at the notion of a "Good Samaritan," but in Jesus' day there was such great hatred toward the Samaritans by Jews that the effect of His description would have been as unsettling as a present-day reference to a Good Terrorist.

Understood in its context, the notion of a Good Samaritan was as unsettling as the notion of a Good Terrorist is today.

The interpretation of a passage must fit the historical-cultural situation of the book. It is more important to reconstruct the historical context than figure out the precise historical date. Use of tools such as a good Bible handbook can help you seek to fulfill the following interpretive goals (adapted from A. Berkeley Mickelsen, *Interpreting the Bible*):

- Know the people or peoples who are involved in the passage being interpreted.
- Determine what time period is the most likely.
- Check the place or places on a map.
- Note the customs, objects of material culture, or social-religious relationships that are in the story.
- Recognize how the history that took place before the times of the original hearers or readers influenced their responses and attitudes.
- Note not just similarities but also differences between the biblical story and the surrounding history and culture.
- Note similarities or differences in the degrees of precision and accuracy customary in matters of measurement and expression between the world of the biblical writer and readers in today's technical-scientific culture.
- Be aware of both similarities and differences between the historical-cultural situation of the original writer and readers, and your own historical-cultural situation (p. 176).

Word Meanings

Each word has a range of meanings. For example, the English word "trunk" may refer to the main stem of a tree, a large piece of luggage, an elephant's nose, a person's torso, or the luggage compartment of an automobile. Also, words change meaning over time. The word that the King James Version translated several times in 1611 as "conversation" does not refer to "people talking" as we mean today; instead, it meant "manner of life" or "conduct." We must be sure the words we read in our Bible mean the same thing today. One of the easiest ways of doing this is to compare how different translations of the Bible treat a given word.

Which words merit more detailed study? Words that you don't understand, words that seem central to what the author is saying, and any words that are repeated or given special emphasis.

How do you study a word? First, determine the word's range of meaning. Bible encyclopedias discuss many important terms. Bible dictionaries shed much light on the meaning and usage of biblical words. Two good ones that do not require a knowledge of Greek and Hebrew are *Vine's Complete Expository Dictionary of Old and New Testament Words* and the *Nelson's New Illustrated Bible Dictionary*, edited by Ronald F. Youngblood. These tools give you the views of the scholars who wrote them. An exhaustive concordance of the Bible translation you choose will enable you to examine all uses of a given word. A concordance lists every word in the Bible in alphabetical order, and the order in which it appears in the Bible. It is probably the most common Bible study tool a person will use in studying the Bible. Thomas Nelson publishes several editions of the *New Strong's Exhaustive Concordance,* but you need to be aware that James Strong based his work on the King James Version.

After considering the possible meanings of the word, choose the meaning that best fits the immediate context. Check your study by reading a good commentary or two on the subject after you have finished your preliminary study.

Grammar

We must pay attention to grammar as well, because words are put together to convey meaning according to rules of grammar. For example, in Ephesians 5:18, Paul exhorted the believers not to get drunk on wine (and be under its influence) but instead to "be filled with the Spirit." The use of the passive voice (rather than the active "fill yourself with the Spirit") indicates that the believer, rather than controlling himself, yields himself to the authority of the Spirit.

The biblical languages (Hebrew for the Old Testament, Greek for the New Testament) sometimes convey subtle meanings not found in English translations. For this reason, it is helpful to consult one or two good commentaries after doing one's own study of the passage.

FAQ #40

What Are the Guidelines for Interpreting Specific Kinds of Literature?

Each kind of literature has its own rules for correct interpretation.

Formal Instruction

Relatively straightforward presentation of the truth characterizes formal instruction, or *didactic* (meaning "to teach") literature. The highly organized explanation moves logically from point to point. Brief books using this literary form are often good starting points for learning personal Bible study skills because their meaning is usually easy to understand.

Paul's explanation of the gospel in Romans is a good example of formal instruction (didactic literature). Paul ties his argument together with the frequent use of transitional and connective words (such as *and, but, for,* and *therefore*) and of rhetorical questions (for example, 2:17-21, 26; 3:1, 3, 5; 4:1, 3, 9). Other biblical examples of the didactic form include the remaining epistles of Paul, as well as Hebrews; 1 and 2 Peter; 1, 2, and 3 John; and Jude.

Study the logical development of the argument.

The most important principle in interpreting this type of literature is to study the logical development of the argument. Try to understand the outline inherent in the chapter. As a second guideline, study the situation behind the statements. Each epistle arose out of and was intended for a specific first-century A.D. occasion. Understanding this occasion will help you to accurately perceive what particular passages meant to their original recipients as well as to validly apply their teachings today. If it is not apparent to you in your study, a good commentary will help.

Narration

Narrative literature emphasizes storytelling to relate a theological message. The Bible's continuing popularity results in part from the many fascinating stories in it. The first book of the Bible, Genesis (a name which means "Beginnings"), relates such stories as how God began the world, the Flood and Noah's ark, the tower of Babel, how God began His plan to bless all people through the family of Abraham, and how He worked in the lives of the Hebrew patriarchs, Abraham, Isaac, Jacob, and Joseph. The second book, Exodus, picks up the story of this family, which has now become the nation of Israel, by telling how Moses leads them out of slavery in Egypt. The Old Testament books from Genesis through Ezra, the four Gospels, and Acts are classified as narrative literature. Stories, such as the one recorded in Isaiah 6, occur in many other books as well.

As you read narrative literature, pay close attention to the plot. How does the story progress? Is the movement of the book primarily physical, spiritual, relational, geographical, or political? What has changed by the end of the book? Why? Pay attention to the contributions of the characters and setting (time, geography, and social customs) to the plot. What theological truth(s) is the author attempting to convey through his selection of material? How might those truths be reflected in people's lives in our time and culture?

Pay close attention to the story's progress, to what changes and why.

The Parable

Not everything in the Gospels belongs to the extended narrative form. The Gospels record many instances of Christ's use of the *parable* in order to teach. A typical definition of a parable is "a saying or story that seeks to drive home a point the speaker wishes to emphasize by illustrating it from a familiar situation of common life" (F. F. Bruce, *Zondervan Pictorial Encyclopedia of the Bible*, 4:590). The word parable refers to several different figures of speech. The form Jesus used most frequently in His teachings is the story-parable. All parables, regardless of form, seek to communicate a spiritual truth by illustrating it with a situation with which the hearer was familiar.

Jesus' explanation of His use of parables (Matthew 13:11-15; Mark 4:10-12) indicates that He had two essential purposes. First, He was attempting to reveal truth to believers. Second, He was trying to conceal the truth from those whose hearts were already hardened against it.

Poetry and Proverbs

Poetry is found mainly in the books of Job, Psalms, Proverbs, Ecclesiastes, and Song of Solomon. However, poetry is scattered throughout other books. Hebrew poetry falls into three categories:

Understanding thought parallelism is the key to understanding all biblical poetry.

1. *Lyric poetry*—to be accompanied by music, like a song

2. *Instructional poetry*—to teach principles of living through pithy maxims

3. *Dramatic poetry*—to tell a story in poetic form

Hebrew poets used two main literary devices: parallelism, the matching of ideas; and figures of speech, or word pictures.

Parallelism. Rather than matching sounds, a Hebrew poet was more concerned with matching ideas. Six of the more common forms of parallelism are:

1. *Synonymous parallelism,* which presents similar ideas:
"Show me Your ways, O Lord;
Teach me Your paths" (Psalm 25:4);

2. *Synthetic parallelism,* **in which the second idea completes the first one:**
   "The Lord is my shepherd;
   I shall not want" (Psalm 23:1);

3. *Antithetic parallelism,* **in which the second thought contrasts with the first:**
   "For the Lord knows the way of the righteous, But the way of the ungodly shall perish" (Psalm 1:6);

4. *Emblematic parallelism,* **where the first line uses a figure of speech to illustrate the idea stated in the second line:**
   "As the deer pants for the water brooks,
   So pants my soul for You, O God" (Psalm 42:1);

5. *Climactic parallelism,* **where the second line repeats the first with the exception of the last word or words:**
   "It is not for kings, O Lemuel,
   It is not for kings to drink wine" (Proverbs 31:4);

6. *Formal parallelism,* **in which the lines of poetry must all exist for a complete thought:**
   "Yet I have set My King
   On My holy hill of Zion" (Psalm 2:6).

Figures of Speech. Since the Hebrew poets wanted mental pictures to pop into the reader's mind, creating visual images was of prime consideration. They accomplished this with vivid figures of speech. Five of the most common figures of speech are

1. *Simile,* **which compares two unlike things:**
   "Keep me as the apple of Your eye" (Psalm 17:8);

2. *Metaphor,* a comparison in which one thing is said to be another:
   "The Lord is my shepherd" (Psalm 23:1);

3. *Hyperbole,* which deliberately overstates for the sake of emphasis:
   "All night I make my bed swim;
   I drench my couch with my tears"
   (Psalm 6:6);

4. *Rhetorical question,* which asks a question for the purpose of making a statement:
   "Who can utter the mighty acts of the LORD,
   Who can declare all His praise?" (Psalm 106:2);

5. *Personification,* which assigns the characteristics of a human to lifeless objects:
   "The sun knows its going down" (Psalm 104:19).

If the reader keeps parallelism and figures of speech in mind when interpreting poetic literature, he understands this poetry much more readily.

Prophecy

Much of the Bible is prophetic. However, prophecy is not just the *foretelling* of the future; it is also the *forthtelling* of God's message to His people. In the Old Testament, the books from Isaiah to Malachi are prophetic; in the New Testament, the Book of Revelation is prophetic. Interpreting prophetic literature can be extremely difficult because so much symbolic, figurative, and non-literal material fills it, and we are not always told what the literal reality is behind the figurative language. A few guidelines, however, help greatly.

First, as with any passage in the Bible, study its history, context, and literal meaning. Study the historical circumstances of both the prophet and the people to whom he prophesied. Carefully consider both the immediate and broad contexts. Take the words in their normal sense unless a figure of speech or a symbol is evidently being used, or unless the passage just doesn't make sense when taken literally. For example, Revelation talks of stars falling to the earth, and stars could not fall to the earth without obliterating it. So the stars must mean something other than literal stars.

Next, identify to whom the passage is written or the subject of the passage. Is the passage forthtelling or foretelling? Has the prophecy been fulfilled? If it has been, study the writings that tell about the fulfillment. Is it unfulfilled? If so, study it carefully and humbly. Unfulfilled prophecy is often very mysterious because of its use of symbolism. Since prophecy is so difficult, prophecy teachers can be helpful, but they can also be confusing, since not all teachers agree on what symbolic language means. Different "schools" of opinion bring various perspectives to Bible prophecy, and it can be challenging but rewarding to become educated in this area.

Finally, remember that the main purpose of prophecy is not to inspire debate, tickle our curiosity, or fuel our opinions. Rather, its purpose is to encourage faith in God and to encourage holy living. For example, Paul introduces his discussion of the future (1 Thessalonians 4:13-18) by saying that he did not want the Thessalonian believers to be ignorant or to grieve as those who have no hope. In contrast to false teachers who evidently were teaching that their loved ones who died before Christ's return would not be raised to new life, Paul proclaimed that "the dead in Christ will rise first" (v. 16), and all believers "shall always be with the Lord. Therefore comfort one another with these words" (vv. 17-18).

Prophey both *forth*tells and *fore*tells.

God desires the promise of Christ's return to have a motivating and purifying effect on the personal life and ministry of Christians (see Titus 2:11-14), and not for its timing to become a source of conflict and division. Therefore, when you study biblical prophecy, always ask yourself, "How does God intend this truth to change my life?"

THINKING BACK

As we have said, the meaning of a given passage in the Bible is not always clear to us. There are three reasons. First, we bring to the interpretation certain assumptions that might not be correct. Second, a great gap of time, culture, and language results in some things written in the Bible being perfectly clear to the ones to whom it was written, and perfectly incomprehensible to us two or three thousand years later. Finally, all communication needs to be interpreted. I have even read things that I have written, and I no longer know what I meant by them. How much more might I be confused by someone else's writing! Oral language is usually accompanied by facial expressions, and vocal inflections. But you do not have these clues to interpretation with the written word. Therefore, when trying to master the word of God so that the word of God can master us, we must work hard at discovering what the Bible says and what it means.

Holy living not curiosity, is the life aim of prophecy.

SPEED BUMP!

1. Why is interpretation necessary?
Interpretation is necessary because it is not always clear to us what a biblical writer meant by what he wrote.

2. What can help me interpret the Scriptures?
Certain principles of interpretation must be followed for any passage of Scripture.

3. What are the guidelines for interpreting specific kinds of literature?
Each kind of literature has its own rules for correct interpretation.

FAQ #41

 Why Is Application So Important?

 Application is important because God expects us not only to know the Bible, but to live it.

Joshua 1:8 says:

This Book of the Law shall not depart from your mouth, but you shall meditate in it day and night, that you may observe to do according to all that is written in it. For then you will make your way prosperous, and then you will have good success.

Several important observations can be made about this passage. First, the book of the Law is not to depart from our mouths, meaning we are to talk about it regularly. But if we talk about it regularly, we must think about it regularly (you shall meditate on it day and night). We will never talk about the word unless we are thinking about the word. Those important observations should encourage us to read, study, memorize, meditate on, and talk about the Bible. However, that is not enough for success in life. Success, as this passage declares, is not a matter of talking about the word, thinking about the word, and knowing the word. Success results from doing the word (that you may observe to do according to all that is written in it). Only as we obey the word do we have the promise that our way will be prosper-

> What makes the difference is not how many times you have been through the Bible, but how many times and how thoroughly the Bible has been through you.
>
> *Gypsy Smith*

ous, and that we will have good success.

The night before His death, Jesus told His apostles, "If you know these things, blessed are you if you do them" (John 13:17). James 1:22-25 both reinforces and expands upon these words:

Do not merely listen to the word, and so deceive yourselves. Do what it says. Anyone who listens to the word but does not do what it says is like a man who looks at his face in a mirror and, after looking at himself, goes away and immediately forgets what he looks like. But the man who looks intently into the perfect law that gives freedom, and continues to do this, not forgetting what he has heard, but doing it—he will be blessed in what he does (NIV).

On the other hand, from God's perspective, knowledge without obedience is sin. James 4:17 states, "Therefore, to him who knows to do good and does it not, to him it is sin." Furthermore, if you don't act on your spiritual understanding and insight, you lose it (Matthew 13:12-15). This was the problem of the believers who were addressed in Hebrews 5:11-14. Although they had had plenty of time to become spiritually mature and become teachers, they were instead spiritual infants because they had not been applying the truth which they had "learned." Fortunately, obedience to the truth leads to increased spiritual insight and growth: "For whoever has, to him more will be given, and he will have abundance" (Matthew 13:12).

Remember that in the New Testament, God desires that His word be written on our hearts, meaning that "our innermost being takes on the character of Scripture, which is the character of God himself. From God's heart to Scripture to our hearts is the divinely intended sequence" (Jack

The Bible is not for satisfying curiosity, but for changing lives.

Kuhatschek, *Taking the Guesswork out of Applying the Bible*, p. 25).
Although total character transformation will not occur until we see
Christ face-to-face (1 John 3:1-3), the process has already begun.

FAQ #42

Why Is Application So Difficult?

**Application is difficult because spiritual growth
takes time and because the world, our innate
pull toward sin, and the devil all militate
against it.**

Some parts of the Bible seem irrelevant to our lives today. Other
sections we don't even understand. Still other portions are under-
standable and sound good when we hear a preacher expound on
them, but when we try to live them, the reward of spiritual growth
happens so slowly that we lose concentration or motivation. Yet the
Bible does pertain to today, and obedience to it honors God. Jesus
asserted, "Whoever has my commands and obeys them, he is the one
who loves me. He who loves me will be loved by my Father, and I too
will love him and show myself to him" (John 14:21 NIV). In 1
Corinthians 10:6, Paul referred to the wilderness wanderings of Israel
(recorded in Exodus and Numbers) when he stated, "these things
became our examples, to the intent that we should not
lust after evil things as they also lusted." He extended
the point to the whole Old Testament in Romans
15:4 when he declared, "For everything that was
written in the past was written to teach us, so that
through endurance and the encourage-
ment of the Scriptures we might have
hope" (NIV).

Second Timothy 3:16-17 proclaims,
"All Scripture is God-breathed and is useful for
teaching, rebuking, correcting and training in right-

eousness, so that the man of God may be thoroughly equipped for every good work" (NIV). All Scripture is both inspired and relevant.

This fact does not mean that every single verse will have dramatic significance for us. When I was attending a Christian college, shortly after my conversion, great attention was given to Isaiah 3:21 as a prime verse for classes which required Scripture memory. It says, simply, "finger rings, nose rings." Admittedly, that verse could not be expected to dramatically impact a high percentage of readers. However, the verse numberings in our present Bible were not in the original writings. The point is, every sentence or every verse is part of a larger unit of thought which is inspired and has some relevance for us.

Scripture sometimes seems irrelevant because it is so specific to the people to whom it was written, and their situations, questions, and concerns are not always our situations, questions, and concerns. However, the Bible is not only timely, it is also timeless with an eternal relevance.

FAQ #43

How Can We Apply the Bible?

We can apply the Bible by studying it diligently, taking its teachings seriously, and committing ourselves to do all that we understand of what God wants of us.

Howard and William Hendricks aptly comment, "Observation plus interpretation without application equals abortion. In other words, every time you observe and interpret but fail to apply, you perform an abortion on the Scriptures in terms of their purpose" (*Living by the Book,* pp. 283–284). At this step in the process of Bible study you ask questions such as: How should my life change as a result of the truth(s) in a particular text? What must I do? What must I believe?

Ask yourself the questions Howard and William Hendricks suggest:

- Is there an example to follow?
- a sin to avoid?
- a promise to claim?
- a prayer to repeat?
- a command to obey?
- a condition to meet?
- an error to mark? or
- a challenge to face? (p. 304)

The key to application involves discovering in a text "the spiritual, moral, or theological principles that have relevance for the contemporary believer" (Henry A. Virkler, *Hermeneutics* p. 212).

As Kuhatschek points out, Jesus Himself emphasized the importance of understanding the general principles that lie behind specific biblical teachings (pp. 52–54). The Jewish rabbis had counted 613 commandments in the Law of Moses. These teachers debated whether some commands were greater in the sense that obeying them necessarily entailed obedience of the "lesser commandments." When Jesus was asked which of the commandments was greatest, He responded:

"'Love the Lord your God with all your heart and with all your soul and all your mind.' This is the first and greatest commandment. And the second is like it: 'Love your neighbor as yourself.' *All the Law and the Prophets hang on these two commandments*" (Matthew 22:37-39 NIV, emphasis mine).

In other words, the commands to love God and others were general principles under which the other 611 laws could be placed. These other 611 commandments gave specific instructions on what to do to love God and what to do to love your neighbor as yourself.

Some specifics of how to express love in our society will differ. For example, Leviticus 19:9-10 commands: "When you reap the harvest of your land, do not reap to the very edges of your field or gather the gleanings of your harvest. Do not go over your vineyard a second time or pick up the grapes that have fallen. Leave them for the poor and the alien" (NIV). These commands limited the wasting of food and made it possible for the physically able but poor to obtain food through personal effort. Although this would be difficult to do today, we can find ways of obeying the spirit of this command.

How can we know whether the original commandments are universal principles that bind us today? While no formula guarantees a correct answer, the following questions are helpful.

1. *Is the passage general or specific?* **Does it apply to everyone, or just to the person to whom it was written, as when Paul wrote to Timothy to "bring the cloak that I left with Carpus at Troas when you come—and the books, especially the parchments" (2 Timothy 4:13). That is a clearly specific command which we don't need to obey. But we might see a more practical principle behind this specific injunction, namely that practical measures that meet physical needs result in genuine and important ministry.**

2. *Does the passage pertain only to a cultural issue of the day, or does it also apply today?* **For example, commands not to eat things offered to idols would be relevant to very few people in the Western world today.**

3. *Has the passage been superseded by a newer or broader teaching?* **For example, the Old Testament command to keep Saturday holy does not apply to us today, because the**

New Testament example was to meet on the first day of the week-Sunday (1 Corinthians 16:2; Acts 20:7).

4. *If the passage clearly states a universal truth and that truth is reiterated, then we are to obey it today.* For example, the Ten Commandments tell us not to murder, and the New Testament repeats the command. This makes it pretty clear that we are not to murder!

5. *Some passages clearly apply to us today, and some passages clearly won't.* Many others can be legitimately debated. We need to understand that and not be discouraged if we waver over a given passage.

To apply *Old Testament commands*, consider first whether the command was either restated or revoked in the New Testament. We no longer need to follow revoked commands. For example, Christ's once-for-all sacrifice fulfilled the Old Testament sacrificial laws (Hebrews 9–10). However, nine of the Ten Commandments are restated in the New Testament, so they are binding today. What about commands that are not directly restated or revoked, such as the commandment to keep the Sabbath? In these cases, consider the principle behind the law. For example, in addition to attending church worship services you might set aside time(s) during the week for rest and special reflection upon God and His goodness to you.

To apply most *New Testament commands*, simply follow the general guidelines for application discussed above. After you understand the

Why I Need to Know This

Observation and interpretation are worthless unless they result in application. Therefore, I need to regard application as critically important to the Christian life, and must also understand how to make effective applications from the Bible.

original circumstances, determine if yours is identical or comparable to it. If your condition is the same, you can apply the command directly. If the situation is not identical, determine the principle behind the command and apply it to situations you face.

What about biblical *examples*? How do we know what to emulate and what to avoid? When the Bible explicitly holds someone up as an example, note whether the author presents the person as a positive or negative example and what is said about him. When the Bible is not explicit about whether a person is a good or bad example and in what respects, then you must evaluate their stories based on truths or principles taught elsewhere in Scripture.

Nine of the Ten Commandments are restated in the New Testament.

Finally, how do you determine how to validly apply biblical *promises*? First, is the promise part of the Old Covenant or the New Covenant? If the former, the promise may not directly apply to us. For example, in Malachi 3:10, we read, "Bring all the tithes into the storehouse, that there may be food in My house, and try Me now in this," says the Lord of hosts, "if I will not open for you the windows of heaven and pour out for you such blessing that there will not be room enough to receive it."

This is often used today as a promise that if we will but tithe our money, God will return abundant material wealth to us. However, this promise was given to the nation of Israel under the Mosaic law. That law was fulfilled in Jesus, and the commands of it are not transferred to the church. The church is certainly instructed to give financial support to the work of the Lord (2 Corinthians 8–9), but nowhere are we instructed in the New Testament to bring food into the house of God (there is no house of God in the New Testament other than believers, in whom God abides, 1 Peter 2:5), and nowhere are we promised material blessing for financial generosity.

Principles from Malachi 3:10 do apply to us today. For example, God rewards obedience (Matthew 5:12; 1 Corinthians 3:14), and we should give back a portion of our income to the Lord as an act of worship and obedience (1 Corinthians 16:1; 2 Corinthians 8–9).

W e cannot expect to receive promises if we refuse to meet their conditions.

If the promise is a New Testament one, then it may or may not apply to us, depending on the answers to other questions. First, to whom is the promise given? As Kuhatschek points out, at least three categories of promises are directly intended for us: those universal in scope (Romans 10:13; 1 John 2:2), those given to the church (Matthew 28:20; Romans 8:28), or those given to other groups to which we belong (Ephesians 6:1–3). When promises are made that were not directly intended for us, we must ask if other Scripture gives us reasons for believing that the promises apply to us in a secondary sense.

We must also ask if the promise is conditional or unconditional. Many promises in the Scripture have at least one condition attached to them. We cannot expect the promise to be given if we do not fulfill the condition. For example, we want God's peace to rule our lives, yet there are clear conditions for this. In Philippians 4:7 we are promised that the peace of God, which surpasses all understanding, will guard our hearts and minds through Christ Jesus. However, the condition for this peace is found in 4:6, "Be anxious for nothing, but in everything by prayer and supplication, with thanksgiving, let your requests be made known to God."

THINKING BACK

Learning how to study the Bible can be a complicated and time consuming process The important thing is not to let the process overwhelm you. When I first became a Christian, the gentleman who led me to the Lord gave me a New Testament and told me to read the Gospel of John six times. Then, I was to start at the beginning and read the entire New Testament. He told me to underline the things I understood and that made sense to me. He encouraged me to write in the margins anything that I needed to change about myself, and then pray to God to help me change it.

Since that time I have had nearly twelve years of formal theological education. I have studied and taught Bible study methods, and am writing a book which includes these methods. My advice for the beginner follows.

First, begin. Start on a level that is meaningful to you, and climb from there as your understanding increases. Since I finished my formal theological education, I have had over twenty years of ministry experience. I still find my original method very fruitful. I read the Bible regularly, concentrating on the things I do understand and know apply to me today. Mark Twain once said something like, "Most people are bothered by the things in the Bible they don't understand. Frankly, the things that bother me are the ones I do understand." I'm the same way. I am still working on "Love the Lord your God with all your heart and with all your soul and with all your mind,...love your neighbor as yourself" (Matthew 22:37-39 NASB). I am still working on "Do not love the world or the things in the world. If anyone loves the world, the love of the Father is not in him. For all that is in the world—the lust of the flesh, the lust of the eyes, and the pride of life—is not of the Father but is of the world" (1 John 2:15-16). I am still working on "I beseech you therefore, brethren, by the mercies of God, that you present your bodies a living sacrifice, holy, acceptable to God, which is your reasonable service. And do not be conformed to this world, but be transformed by the renewing of your mind, that you may prove what is the good and acceptable and perfect will of God" (Romans 12:1-2). I am convinced that if we were faithful to everything that we do understand from the Bible, we would have much less difficulty dealing with the passages we don't understand.

The second thing I advise is to get a good biblical education. The Bible is such an enormous and difficult book that very few of us can gain a good understanding of it without solid Bible teaching. When looking for good teachers, look for two things. First, make sure they are not teaching something entirely new. In the basic body of information that all orthodox Christians have agreed on and believed for the last two thousand years, there is not likely to be something really big and entirely new. These "fundamentals of the faith" need to be foundational in anyone from whom you learn. The fundamentals would include:

- A holy God exists who is the creator of all that is.
- Jesus, the Son of God, is also divine, and came to earth to die for our sins.
- The Holy Spirit is also God, and has an active ministry in our lives today.
- This one God exists eternally in three persons, God the Father, God the Son, and God the Holy Spirit. They are the same in substance but distinct in subsistence. There is no God other than this triune God.
- Humans are separated from God because of their sin, and must be saved from their lost condition since they cannot save themselves. Salvation is available by grace through faith in Jesus Christ. By repenting of our sin and committing our lives to following Jesus, we are given eternal life by God.
- The Bible is the word of God, verbally and totally inspired by God, and without error in the original manuscripts. There is no Scripture but the Bible.
- Christians are to band together in local churches to worship God, to build one another up in the faith, to carry the message of salvation to the world, and to be humanitarians to those in need.
- Jesus is returning someday. We are to give people this hope, warn others of the dangers of dying without Christ, and live in hope and purity of life ourselves.

Concentrate on what you do understand and can apply.

Your Bible teacher should hold to these fundamentals of the faith. He should also be a person of high moral and ethical integrity. A person lax in either morals or ethics is not worthy to be followed as a Bible teacher. Even within these very broad boundaries, there are good Bible teachers and poor ones. The Holy Spirit must guide you as you pray for a good Bible teacher. But remember, you can also be taught by books, audiotapes, videotapes, and television and radio. Wonderful Bible teachers in each of these areas can be of great benefit. Be discerning, because there are also poor Bible teachers in each of these media. Rely heavily on prayer and the guidance of the Holy Spirit. Do not depend entirely on nonpersonal teaching, however, for God never intended us to make it alone. He wants us to become involved in the lives of others who believe as we do.

Study with a good Bible teacher.

Observation, interpretation, and application: Those are the three keys to mastering the Bible and having the Bible master us.

SPEED BUMP!

1. Why is application so important?
Application is important because God expects us not only to know the Bible, but to live it.

2. Why is application so difficult?
Application is difficult because spiritual growth takes time and because the world, our innate pull toward sin, and the devil all militate against it.

3. How can we apply the Bible?
We can apply the Bible by studying it diligently, taking its teachings seriously, and committing ourselves to do all that we understand of what God wants of us.

BIBLIOGRAPHY

Anders, Max E. *30 Days to Understanding the Bible*. Nashville: Thomas Nelson, Inc., 1998. *30 Days to Understanding the Christian Life*. Nashville: Thomas Nelson, Inc., 1998. *30 Days to Understanding What Christian's Believe*. Nashville: Thomas Nelson, Inc., 1998.

Bloom, Allan. *The Closing of the American Mind*. New York: Simon & Schuster, 1987.

Colson, Charles. *Loving God*. Grand Rapids: Zondervan, 1987.

Fee, Gordon D., and Douglas Stuart. *How to Read the Bible for All Its Worth* (2nd ed.). Grand Rapids: Zondervan, 1993.

Frye, Northrop. *The Great Code: The Bible and Literature*. New York: Harcourt, 1983.

Graham, Billy. *How to Be Born Again*. Dallas: Word, Inc., 1989.

Green, Michael P. *Illustrations for Biblical Preaching*. Grand Rapids: Baker Book House Co., 1988.

Hendricks, Howard G., and William D. Hendricks. *Living by the Book*. Chicago: Moody Press, 1993.

Henrichsen, Walter A. *A Layman's Guide to Interpreting the Bible*. Grand Rapids: Zondervan, 1985.

Herriot, James. *All Things Wise and Wonderful*. New York: St. Martin's Press, 1977.

Kennedy, D. James. *"The Bible: Fable, Fraud or Fact."* Coral Ridge Video Ministry (January 4, 1994).

Klein, William W., and Craig L. Bomberg. *Introduction to Biblical Interpretation*. Dallas: Word, Inc., 1993.

Kuhatschek, Jack. *Taking the Guesswork Out of Applying the Bible*. Downer's Grove, IL: InterVarsity Press, 1990.

Lindsell, Harold. *God's Incomparable Word*. Minneapolis: World Wide Publications, 1978.

McDowell, Josh. *New Evidence that Demands a Verdict*. Nashville: Thomas Nelson, Inc, 1999.

Mickelsen, A. Berkeley. *Interpreting the Bible*. Grand Rapids: Eerdmans, 1963.

Mickelsen, A. Berkeley, and Alvera M. Mickelsen. *Understanding Scripture* (rev. ed.). Peabody, MA: Hendrickson Pubs., Inc., 1992.

Packer, James I. *God Has Spoken*. Grand Rapids: Baker Book House

Co., 1994.

Ryken, Leland. "The Literary Influence of the Bible," in *A Complete Literary Guide to the Bible* (eds., Leland Ryken and Tremper Longman III). Grand Rapids: Zondervan, 1993.

Sivan, Gabriel (ed.). *The Bible and Civilization.* New York: Times Books, 1974.

Traina, Robert A. *Methodical Bible Study.* Grand Rapids: Zondervan, 1985.

Virkler, Henry A. *Hermeneutics.* Grand Rapids: Baker Book House Co., 1981.

Wald, Oletta. *The Joy of Teaching Discovery Bible Study* (rev. ed.). Minneapolis: Augsburg, 1975.